River Teeth Literary Nonfiction Prize

SERIES EDITORS:
Daniel Lehman, Ashland University
Joe Mackall, Ashland University

The River Teeth Literary Nonfiction
Prize is awarded to the best work of
literary nonfiction submitted to the
annual contest sponsored by *River
Teeth: A Journal of Nonfiction Narrative.*

AN INSIDE PASSAGE

Kurt Caswell

University of Nebraska Press

Lincoln and London

Manufactured in the United States of America

∞

Some of these essays originally appeared in the following publications: "California Rental" in *Isotope* (spring 2004); "Fawn" in *Northern Lights* (winter 2001); "Letter to a Young Girl at Summer's End" in *Northern Lights* (spring 2003); "A Matter for Heron" in *Boise Magazine* (fall 1998); "Banaue Tercet" in *Matter* 9 (2006); "The Best Thing about Marriage Is Divorce" in *Ninth Letter* (fall–winter 2007); "Wild Man at Iouzan" in *Pilgrimage* 31.3 (2006); "Hunger at the Mountain" in *Janus Head* (spring–summer 2007); "An Inside Passage" in *Matter* 10 (2007).

Library of Congress Cataloging-in-Publication Data

Caswell, Kurt, 1969–
An inside passage / Kurt Caswell.
p. cm. — (River Teeth Literary Nonfiction Prize)
ISBN 978-0-8032-3214-3 (pbk.: alk. paper)
1. Caswell, Kurt, 1969—Travel. 2. Home—Psychological aspects. I. Title.
PS3603.A893Z46 2009
818'.6—dc22
[B]
2008044808

Set in Scala.
Designed by Ashley Muehlbauer.

For Suzanne, who traveled this road

Contents

Acknowledgments

I am grateful to the many people who have supported and guided me in my work, some perhaps without knowing it. I am especially grateful to Curtis Bauer, Sven Birkerts, Matthew Bokovoy, Scott Dewing, John Elder, Idoia Elola, Suzanne Forrester, Debra Gwartney, Kerry Hart, John Hendee, David Huddle, Barry Lopez, Antonio Massella, Jordan Messerer, Alan Minskoff, Robert Pack (whose life and work I admire to the utmost), Laurel Saville, Bob Shacochis, Scott Thompson, Susan Tomlinson, and Laurie Zimmerman.

To my guides and companions who opened the door to the sacred mountain, especially Angelo Lazenka, Emerald North, Robert Wagner, and Jennifer Yamamoto.

My family, certainly, who are a refuge for me: my father and mother, Jim and Susan Caswell; my sisters Rebecca Whitson and Cari Harbaugh; and their families, Wally, Tyler, and Troy; and Chadd, Drew, and Leah. The various dogs and such. My grandmother, Maxine. My uncle, David. And my Danish kin in Michigan, with whom I am recently reacquainted.

I wish to thank the editors of the River Teeth Literary Nonfiction Book Prize for their vision and support of writers and writing, Joe Mackall and Dan Lehman, and also Sarah Wells and Amy Guth. And the good people I've worked with in preparing the final draft of this manuscript, especially Ann Baker, Carolyn Einspahr, Tish Fobben, Ashley Muehlbauer, Ladette Randolph, Kristen Rowley, and Rhonda Winchell at the University of Nebraska Press.

And, finally, to Margo Aragon, who read early drafts of many of these essays and offered invaluable insight and direction. Her friendship and care are in these pages.

An Inside Passage

California Rental

L ate summer blackberries are gone now. The vines have drawn their juices in. And the sunburned grass is oak-leaf strewn, brittle to my every step. Yellow jackets (people here call them "meat bees") cluster like crabs between the window and the screen. And in this stillness waiting, it rains the first rain in weeks on the hour of the equinox.

I walk outside my rented house in the southern Cascade Mountains of northern California, inspecting the ground for black bear tracks near the woodpile; I thought I heard footsteps in the night. I find no bear sign in the rained-fresh earth but there, where reflected light redirects my eye, a small red toy car. I pick it up. It is dense and boxy, foreign and artificial. Who was the child who dropped this here? How long ago? Mother calling? Or haphazardly in pursuit of something else? What life passed through this place in a time just beyond my reach?

These past days since we moved in, my wife and I have unearthed artifacts of other lives, signs of the people who have lived in this house. In the attic storage space I finger thin clay shards scattered on the floor, a potter's fractured labor. A penny in the grass is a hole in someone's pocket? A forgotten box of cat litter (still sporting that smell) beneath the lip of the back deck. We find so much of those who came before it seems the house resists our getting too settled too soon.

Suzanne and I married just days ago. It was a small ceremony in Orofino, Idaho, at my parents' house overlooking the Clearwater River. We try not to trust illusions about how common or how extraordinary our experiences were, or will be. We're new at this, we know.

With our boxes stacked center-high in the living room, we work at the kitchen first, because so much settling comes with settled food. We wipe down the shelves and countertops with a solution of warm water and bleach. We unroll glasses and cups, plates and pie pans from newspaper packing, rewash all of it despite having packed it clean. We load the shelves with this here, that there, making it up as we go.

We clean behind the refrigerator (because it isn't our dirt) and discover the secret web-work of the ubiquitous cellar spider, how many summers old? A Pilot V Ball pen, extra fine, black. A dime, and three pennies. Another pen, ballpoint, with "Advantage 2U Appliance, Shingletown CA" printed on the side; the cap red, white, and blue. And in the deepest corner, a plastic monarch butterfly, its toy wings arcing in forever flight. I hesitate with the humming Shop-Vac in my hand—what right do I have—and then plunge in, sucking up the evidence.

Whose gear this is I do not know, whose lives still linger in the webs. Even in their absence, these former inhabitants make their claim. A disquieting mood washes over me: I am an interloper here, a stranger to this place and this space.

We unpack pictures and artwork for the walls. A framed Robert Bly broadside, "No. 76/250, Six Winter Privacy Poems"; a print of Annie Lee's "Blue Monday"; my treasured shodo piece by my Japanese friend, Mikami; a pencil drawing of the main gate at The Orme School in Arizona, where Suzanne and I met and fell in love. We lean them all against the wall, stacked one in front of the other.

Wandering through the house, we try to picture where our pictures go. "How about this here?" and "How about that there?" we call to each other from different rooms. The walls are peppered with other people's pounded nails inside the sun-faded outlines of former pictures. I guess at them: family portraits, favorite dogs, a daughter's graduation. The house holds onto the memory of these former arrangements. I get my hammer and, one by one, jack the nails out.

But some remembrances can't be removed. The owners, two college professors at the University of California–Chico, are kind, generous people who love this house. They bought two ceramic tiles—one a moon, the other a sun—on a tour through Spain, and mounted them on either end of the shower walls. Bathing is a daily reminder of the first lives embedded in this house.

Still, we're settling in just fine. Cleaning up overlapping lives—in the house and in us. Old relationships to leave behind, old habits, old attitudes are all replaced with taking care of ourselves and each other. This is the way good new beginnings might be.

After our day's work we sit down together, Suzanne and I, on the back deck looking out on Mount Lassen. I open two bottles of local beer— after-work prizes—and watch one of the green caps go willy-nilly across the deck. I bend to catch it but it slips between my fingers and down between the planks. I hear it touch bottom and roll still. Peering down through a crack with one eye, I see it there beneath us, settled in just out of reach. And, beside it, something else: a plastic toy cowboy, stuck upside down in the leaf litter.

I return to the moment: out before us now, the Earth curves away under the sun, settling pink across the mountains. An acorn woodpecker rings in the oak beyond the star thistle. Another leaf falls.

Five Country Walks

When I rest my feet my mind also ceases to function.

J. G. HAMANN

I

Boise, Idaho, USA—1989

I began walking one cloudy day, without ceremony, to while away a Sunday afternoon. The day was warm and moist and early fall, and I pulled on my boots and walked outside. At that time, I lived near the edge of the university campus, and the Boise River was on the far side of it. I set off in that direction, after posting a letter to a woman who would not love me.

My boots were suede leather and nylon, very light, almost a running shoe, and well broken so that I wore them without discomfort. They made no sound in themselves, and very little against the Earth, shaped and rolling in the gait of my walking. Later, in Marseille, France, I would pass them on to an old traveler who said he had been a salvage diver on deep sea wrecks. His shoes were tattered and toe-less, with the soles worn through. I was sporting new boots I'd purchased in Rome. I noticed him eyeing the old boots tied to my pack, asking why or how the world was so geared as to provide me with two pairs of boots and him none. So I evened it out.

Where the path met the river I walked against the current, along the edge of the great asphalt parking lot behind Bronco Stadium. The artificial turf, a brilliant blue, was said to attract waterfowl in winter, ducks and such from the river. But I thought it a silly story, a lie, even, one our culture tells to trick us into believing that the artificial is as good as the natural.

The path passed beneath the bridge on Broadway—usually busy with commuters and consumers, but quieter on Sundays—and on out beyond the business district, where a number of large corporations had set up shop headquarters. I wound through the cottonwood trees wrapped in chain-link fence against the beaver, and on up, a cyclist whizzing by, a runner pushing a baby in a big-wheeled stroller, and a mallard and a merganser at slow tread in the river eddies.

I paused at the outdoor theater of the Idaho Shakespeare Festival (which isn't held there anymore). The summer before, I had seen a Shakespeare play, *Troilus and Cressida*, for the first time, with a friend who was both an actor and a teacher. Although the production did not wow me—the Greeks dressed in Hell's Angels costumes, the Trojans in Frederick's of Hollywood—the experience was freeing: Shakespeare's language with wine and fresh bread on the public lawn before I was of age.

There were no locks or doors of any kind, so I entered the theater, stage left. I stood at center stage looking out on the tiny plot of green grass (it had been so much larger during the play). The theater space was painted a forest green, almost black, edged with columns against the spare plywood background. I climbed up onto the catwalk to take in the view from the actor's position, came back down, and then, standing center stage, delivered my lines to the empty sky: "To be, or not to be, that is the question . . ." and on, as far as I could remember it. Then I turned and made my exit.

The asphalt pathway led me on, greenery on both sides, behind a building made of mirrors. Was anyone inside looking out? The way became a bridge over a creek flowing into the main river, and two pairs of mallard duck, male and female, flew up out of the water in front of me, so close I might have touched them if I'd tried.

And fast around the corner, a runner, a woman, came out of the future, charging by. I felt the heat of her heart as she passed, and my surging desire now cooling on the riparian after-moment.

The path made two more turns and I broke out of the trees and the city and into the drier, sandy desert country more typical of southern Idaho. The asphalt turned to earth, and the path became a boot-worn track following the bending water.

I wanted to check my watch, to see if I had been walking long enough for anything to happen. I resisted, stretching myself out longer, farther than I wanted to go. Instead of leading me into forgotten country as I had expected, the path turned again into the world. The earthen footpath transformed to asphalt. I passed a complex of apartments and a series of ritzy homes at riverside. Was there no good country left? Would the entire riverside be paved to still the sound of questions on an earthen path?

I stopped and descended the bank to the moving water. The surface of it swirled and softened away. I placed my hands in the cold current, my fingers like eyes over the smooth bottom stones. I lifted one out and turned it over to a dozen Jurassic creatures escaping into my hands. I set the stone back down gently.

My hands were cold in the warmer air. I put them into the water again to remember this difference. I thought I would go. The sun was getting on in years and it would be dark soon. I waited a moment more, until a great blue heron hidden by stillness rose up from the river's edge and pulled and tucked and smoothed away as it faded against the river and the close of day.

Back in my little apartment, seated with afternoon coffee and a book, I realized I was still walking, I was still out traveling, when I came to these lines:

As a general rule of biology, migratory species are less "aggressive" than sedentary ones.

There is one obvious reason why this should be so. The migration itself, like the pilgrimage, is the hard journey: a "leveller" on which the "fit" survive and stragglers fall by the wayside.

The journey thus pre-empts the need for hierarchies and shows of dominance. The "dictators" of the animal kingdom are those who live in an ambience of plenty. The anarchists, as always, are the "gentle-men of the road."

BRUCE CHATWIN, *The Songlines*

II

Chitose, Hokkaido, Japan—1994

Lake Shikotsu formed inside a collapsed volcanic caldera; the water is deep and cold. The local people call it Dead Bones Lake because the bottom is said to be a wide plain of suicides. The Chitose River flows out from here, and follows and creates the green wet overgrowth of the little valley. It meets the Ishikari River to the northeast and flows down and out into the Japan Sea.

I live here with the birds: the birds I know and the birds I don't know. Kawasemi, the common kingfisher, a little nomad, here only in spring and summer, maybe early fall when the salmon run; hashibuto-garasu, the jungle crow, the big black-feathered feeder, often confused with the northern raven; ao-sagi, or sagi, as people here call it, the grey heron, also a migratory bird, following at the river's edge, the fish and frogs. And there are others.

At 10:00 a.m. almost every morning I leave my small apartment at Kasuga-cho 2-chome and walk over the footbridge into Aoba Park. The walking path here leads through the lush northern woods and out into the sporting fields for baseball (a recent Japanese obsession), soccer, rugby, and play spaces for children, with a central fountain. Moving through these trees the ground is moist with summer dew, the path, foot-worn wood chips following the perimeter of the park.

Twenty years ago this park was wild country. My friend, Takuji Noguchi, a haberdasher in Chitose, used to play here as a boy. He said in those days these woods were alive with spirits. He would run among the trees as fast as he could, in joy and terror, with a dozen demons on his tail. It was, he said, the best time of his life.

Walking here I meet old men, bald headed with the folds of time draw-ing their faces down. One fellow I meet almost every day carries a long staff across his lower back with his arms bent over it at the elbows. He walks this way to keep his posture, I guess, his composure, his compas-sion? I do not know. We exchange only smiles as we pass.

When fall leaves fall, salmon come up the river to leave their progeny and their bodies behind. And crow is here rejoicing in mealtime along the salmon-littered shores.

On some walks I'll go upriver beyond the park entrance, beyond the little cars that go whizzing by in the early morning, past country people headed into town. I'll go on up around the shape of the river shaping the land, a kawasemi's sharp call at Doppler play in my ears. I come to the place the river drops over a ledge and plunges into a roiling hole, the place Noguchi and I come to play at surfing in canoes. I pause, remembering rivers I have run in Idaho and Oregon: the Payette, the Deschutes, the Middle Fork of the Salmon. Scenes of this place, too, past weeks and months with Noguchi going over this little drop, backward and forward, spilling out in our canoes and rolling back up, paddles splayed high, laughter, and fast the faster water draws beneath the boat and surges and plays and fattens as it speeds.

It was up here, somewhere in the country of the river, that the same woman I loved back in that time of Idaho stumbled on the body of a man who had hung himself in a maple tree. We tried to live together in Hokkaido, and that day we had quarreled, so far from home. She went out to ride her bike for sanctuary. She returned trembling like a leaf, and I held her heaving steady as she cried and told me about the hanging-man she'd found. I felt her strength then in her weakness, her sorrow, and knew again the shock adolescents find in the exchange of the imagination for adult reality. She praised me for my compassion, my willingness to listen, and she kissed me and told me what a good person, what a good man, what a good husband I would make some day, for someone else.

Later she talked about the hung-man's face, the hands and bare feet, purple like lupine blossoms, the way the Japanese police were more interested in her—a beautiful blonde foreigner—than the tragedy in the tree. As it turned out, the dead man was the city's chief of education and the husband of a student of mine. The woman, his wife, fell from public approval and vanished. She told me which tree it was that she found him in, which branch, where he lay when they cut him down, and how he fell and lay like a sack of rice. And now, forever, in that place and time, that tree bears the weight of it, and in our memories, too, and so do we hold it between us: a force of attraction, a force of repulsion.

But the river moves on from here, and that place and that tree have both grown but not been forgotten. I doubt if I will ever go back.

The path along Chitose River, each stopping place, I will always know as mine: the bridge with brass birds that sing in electric warblings when you pass, the Shinto shrine at the top of the hill, and the riverbend behind the community center where the water swirls in a wide eddy and I go to skip stones. Here, in the morning, I found the silvered bodies of a dozen tiny trout laid up on the rocks and carelessly abandoned to the jungle crows. But the jungle crows have not been keeping up with their work, else I would not find them here at all, these lost pages from the river's story. I cradled each one in my hands and let them out easily on the back of the river. Like petals they swirled away.

After (it was over) my lover flew home to America, I came here with another woman local to this place. She would go a-wandering into the woods with me, and walk behind me when we walked, and behind just a bit more until I could no longer see or sense her and I found I was walking alone. I would call her name into the foreign trees and wait to hear, but no reply, only the wind at play in the dwarf bamboo. I walked along, calling for her, until she, in a burst of giggles and smiles, would appear out of the forest like a dark fairy from my dreams.

One rainy afternoon we set out on the path to the headwaters of Naibetsugawa, a feeder stream off the main river from which the town gets its drinking water. The place is a spring, a pooling source emerging from the deep Earth. We found the old road there, cut years ago to get the timber out, but long since fallen to disuse. We could expect to be alone. Basho said it best: "None is traveling / Here along this way but I— / This autumn evening."

The air grew colder, sharper as we walked, and we came to a crossing where the creek broadened into a pool. It began to snow. I looked up through the trees at the sky to ask if we should go on. We hadn't come dressed for the weather. But she, unafraid, took a long bamboo leaf and folded it into a tiny boat. She took my hand and we knelt and set it free on the moving water. We watched it cross the pool, ride the little waves and burble around the rocks, tumble down beyond where we could see it—perhaps it would make it to the ocean!

She taught me how to fold the boats, and then we made more and let them go. We set two adrift at once, to race. Shoulder to shoulder we waited like children, as first hers, then mine, then finally hers came out ahead. We made more boats and let them go, and at one time we had nine boats at sail on the water, and watched them slip one by one over the edge of the pool.

We did not have far to go and the snow was a comfort now, so we walked on, covering the distance in under an hour. She played her hiding game, disappearing into the forest and returning again in flurries of girlish laughter. She took my hand and skipped along beside me under the horsetail swinging of her long black hair; I felt that young, too.

The road softened into the next turn and without warning we came to the end of it. The spring was there, the water coming up in an Oh!, black and deep and beautiful. How far, how deep we could go if we stripped our clothes and plunged deep down, diving, as deep as the Earth would take us. And would we find God down there, or the devil?

The pool invited us. We knelt side by side on the wet ground, soaking our knees, humbled our heads, and drank like cats. We loved each other then, and the evening would become the morning in the rising sun wrapped in each others arms.

> Above all do not lose your desire to walk: every day I walk myself into a state of well-being and walk away from every illness; I have walked myself into my best thoughts, and I know of no thought so burdensome that one cannot walk away from it . . . but by sitting still, and the more one sits still, the closer one comes to feeling ill . . . Thus if one just keeps on walking, everything will be all right.
>
> SOREN KIERKEGAARD, letter to Jette, 1847

III

Borrego Pass, New Mexico, USA—1995

At Borrego Pass School on the Navajo Reservation, 8,000 feet above the sea, I walked first alone and then with the dog, a Queensland I called Kuma. He came to live with me at five weeks old and I always felt it was a bit too soon to leave his mother. His ears did not go up, bat-like, the way they should have, and his temperament was wary, aggressive, deeply pessimistic. But he loved (or hated?) Mozart. I played all kinds of music for him to which he paid no mind. But when I played Mozart, and especially the overture to *Le Nozze de Figaro*, he would raise his ears, cock his head, and sing and howl and wail as if calling on angels or devils, I wasn't sure. He was a good dog despite his love for fighting and herding cars and trucks on the dirt road and biting whatever or whoever crossed him. I was in need of a companion in those days, so we loved each other in that time.

I went walking out through the fields of late-fall desert flowers, the yucca and stunted piñon pine, the soft sandstone labyrinth. Out here there would be no water, and I usually carried none. It was a moderate risk, as my old rented trailer at the school where I worked was never more than a few miles away and in this open country it was easy to get around.

I happened upon Manny one day, behind the water tower where the rock face rises sharply. A sixth-grade Zuni student in this otherwise all-Navajo school, he was soft and round, a little shy. He carried a CO_2 pistol in his hand, and three colorful birds that were stuffed head first into his pants pocket. He explained, without a prompter: My uncle's gonna use the feathers.

Merle Moore, and his wife Rosie, managers of the Borrego Pass Trading Post, kept their cattle on this range, long-legged creatures that could live on rocks and sand. The dog and I would find places trampled out by cows, and in their wake, minefields of beautiful green bovine splats. Being the kind of dog he was, Kuma was always more titillated than I.

Ranging as far as we could go, out from the school, out through the rolling desert around the mesa foot and beyond, passing some forgotten hogan where an ol' Navajo had died. Just at the edge of as far as I could see, the Christian cemetery, without entrance or perimeter. The only definition was the stones themselves. A quiet little place of not so many plots, and only one or two stones still standing.

I wandered among the markers, over the bodies laid to rest so close beneath the ground. I moved in and out, back and forth, reading the names and dates. On they went, dry and forgotten, these stones, these lives, lying face-up to the Navajo sun.

One tree, one little pine, grew on the southern end of the cemetery, just outside the stones. And against it a rusted shovel, about four feet long. The handle too was steel, the end of it split to accept a steel handhold welded in. Since I didn't have a shovel in my truck to dig myself out should it rain, I shouldered this one, worrying all the way back that it may have been used to bury the dead.

On one of my desert walks I made my way out across the flatlands under the shadow of a red-tailed hawk that followed quite a distance and then disappeared against the cirrus clouds. Kuma was still a pup then, and he had not grown into his later knowledge of cactus beds. I stopped to rescue him from the middle of a wide patch of needles, where any direction he went was a painful teacher. I turned him over on my legs in the shade of a ponderosa to pull the spines from his tender puppy feet. He whelped and whimpered against the barbs. Something caught my eye. Just beside me, partially buried in the sandy soil, the bottom of an Anasazi pot, the biggest piece of ancient pottery I had ever found.

I kept on doing what I was doing, watching the pot shard from the side of my eyes until I had cleaned all the harm from my dog's feet. He was better, then, and smarter too, or more worldly, or more wary of the world that bites.

I leaned over on my elbow near the pot shard and brushed the sandy soil back. The piece kept going, deeper and deeper into the ground. I paused. The Navajo do not generally disturb Anasazi relics, I had heard, not out of respect for ancient peoples or wisdom but because they fear retribution by the Anasazi dead. (Later, I would learn that Navajos generally reject this idea.) I wasn't really afraid of ghosts, at least I told myself so, but perhaps to dig deeper was to violate the spirit of the place? Then again, the country around Borrego, indeed most of the American Southwest, was looted by treasure hunters a hundred years ago. So why was I worrying over an old clay chip in some forgotten corner of the desert that every day risked returning to dust beneath the hoof action of Merle's cows?

I brushed more sand back, and where the deeper ground was more solid I used my fingers pressed together like a spade to get down to the rooted edge. It came free. I brushed the dirt from my hands and paused to admire the beauty of the piece. It was as big as both my hands set side by side with my fingers spread wide, and roughly in the shape of Australia. I inspected it closely for fractures. None. The piece was as solid as it was when it was fired seven hundred to two thousand years ago. It was the bottom of a pot, the thicker, tougher part, the place it would have rested on the earth. The outside, an intricate houndstooth pattern. The inside smooth, curved, moist (a little). It sang in my hands with stories of the past. I wanted to keep it.

The dog was gone. I called for him. Nothing. He had likely grown bored and followed his nose to some sun-mutilated skeleton on the sand. I put the piece in my pocket, feeling guilty all the while, and wandered out to call him home. It was time for me to go, too.

On the way, with Kuma safely returned, we traveled across the back of the mesa where we had not been before. We stayed out in the open country for as long as we wished, walking softly and surely among the scattered cows. A light wind blew cross-wise against us, delivering the scent of fresh cow as we walked, so dry was the rhythmic air. We might have gone on around the entire mesa, a long walk that would have taken us behind the trading post and over the hill that Merle claims is the site of some not-so-ancient massacre. Every time it rains, he says, the bones of children wash into his backyard.

I love long walks, but this walk had gone on long enough. The sun was falling into the western lands and I was hungry and thirsty and weathered and ready for something else. So we turned up a little wash that would take us over the mesa again and back to my trailer home.

The wash steepened as we went, the slope on either side coming up around us like ribs over the belly of a great animal. We skirted boulders and roots of pine perched on the edge of life in this rocky, scorpion-tail country, pulling ourselves up by tooth and claw. At one point I hefted first the dog and then myself onto a ledge and crawled across a fallen tree that served as a bridge between us and the crack of doom.

I wondered if we wouldn't get caught inside this canyon and have to go back the long way round, which meant perhaps walking part of it in the dark. But I could see the top now and I thought we'd make it.

Kuma stopped. The hair on his back and tail rose up, and he growled low in his throat. I stopped, too, and crept up behind him cautiously. He nosed the air, pumping his body forward and back in hesitation like a snake, which is what I thought he'd found. But no. Deep in the chasm lay the wreckage of a dead horse.

The lips were laid back from the teeth and the eyes were empty hollows. The neck was twisted up at a too-sharp angle. The legs, broken and bent under the body, seemed to be coming from every direction.

The ribs curved up and around where the insides were no longer. The hide, tanned by the sun, was stiff like wood. There was nothing wet about this death at all.

We read the story in the land: where the horse had broken down, the turning point in the sand, markings of horse feet shuffling across the dirt, skidding here, tripping up there, where the animal lost its balance, sick maybe? or lost and dehydrated into delirium? Old and blind? All of it coming to the edge of these rocks, the edge of its life, in a final effortless grace, it fell in and out of this world. I thought something needed blessing, so I said, "Amen," and then, with Kuma, scrambled up and over the mesa to the other side.

Back at the trailer I discovered that quite nothing had happened in my absence. Everything was as I left it. Did I expect something more? I removed my boots before going in, went in, and shut the door.

Day in and day out, a baby cannot have enough walking. And if babies instinctively demand to be walked, the mother, on the African savannah, must have been walking too: from camp to camp on her daily foraging round, to the waterhole and on visits to the neighbors.

BRUCE CHATWIN, *The Songlines*

IV
Orme Ranch, Mayer, Arizona, USA—1997

I walked an even route up Ash Creek, a dry arroyo much of the year, and up between the three mesas named by Chick Orme in the old days: Little Mesa, Big Mesa, Indian Mesa. On my way I passed under the strong arm of a cottonwood tree spread out over the dirt road. Each time I went walking I expected to see that the massive limb had come down in some summer after-storm. But it never did. Cottonwoods, solid as earth and sky, pulled water up from deep down below, from the Earth's heart inside. In the desert Southwest cottonwoods will show you the way to water.

Kuma was still with me then, and out into the desert grasslands was the only place he could feel free. More and more he could not stomach domestic life, and it did not stomach him. He lashed out at every turn: killed skunks, attacked other dogs, bit at a boy's ankle. I knew what he needed was a herd of cows to work and the space to work them. The Orme Ranch didn't work with cow dogs, and so I would need to find him a ranch that did.

But for now I'd take him out there every day and we'd pass under that great arm of cottonwood marking the edge of the houses on the ranch before the great wild Arizona desert. When I cut him loose from the leash, he never ran back onto the school campus, always out and beyond, always out into open country.

We might begin with the creek, crossing over it first to the dry bank on the other side, then past the old shooting range where students at the ranch school used to target shoot. Story is, students brought their own .22 caliber rifles and stowed them in the shooting instructor's house under lock and key. But all keys can be stolen and all locks broken, and one afternoon a student took his rifle from its place and shot the admissions director in the belly. The admissions director lived; the student did not. People here describe it like this: "The cops did a Dirty Harry on him in the barnyard."

So we went by that place, long since silent, the shooting shack broken in the sun, light flashing from thousands of .22 shells scattered and forgotten.

From here the trail passes over the top of the hill overlooking what is known locally as Indian Kitchen. The hilltop itself is Indian House. These old Sinaguan ruins, the outer stone walls of a living structure up here, a cluster of metate among the immovable basalts down there. Arrow points—you come across them from time to time—lie forgotten in the Arizona soil.

Fields of tsubosa grass roll north and west and south. The edge of the plateau looking south marks the Salt River Valley, the cities of Phoenix and Tucson, and the greater Sonora desert.

When monsoon rains travel through in the fall, the flowers want to bloom again in a second coming: desert globemallow, blue dick, storksbill, sacred datura, chicory, paintbrush, beardtongue and Arizona lupine. Some cacti, too: prickly pear and desert barrel. The acacia or catclaw, and mesquite roll out of the dry washes, entangling anything, dog or man or javelina, that tries to pass. Only the rattlesnake gets through. The cottonwood spread their arms across the sky, a great train of trees up the creek on both sides, thickening as they go. Soon hackberry are here, and desert willow.

I can see in the distance the three mesas against the ranch boundary. "Indian Mesa," because a student at the ranch school found a bow here in the 1950s. It was tucked away in a little volcanic depression, a cave where now I find the dried and withered bones of a cougar-killed pronghorn.

This land, about twenty-five hundred acres of private land and thirty thousand acres of surrounding Forest Service land, has supported cattle for at least 150 years. The Orme family bought the ranch in 1929, and opened the school for their children. The ranch and school now operate independently, and the ranch manager (no longer an Orme) is, contrary to popular stereotypes, one of the most environmentally sound people I know. His sons are both adopted. Their surname is Kessler, like the whiskey, so the oldest boy is Jigger, a shotful of father. The younger brother goes by J. L. B., an acronym for "Jigger's Little Brother." Like their father, the boys are tied to the land, what it needs in response to human engineering, how it responds to personalities and to personal endeavors. In times of drought I have seen this desert-tested family weep for the dying grass.

High away in the distance turkey vultures ride the high currents over Big Mesa. Somewhere out there a spirit has fallen, and the great feeders have come to spread the flesh and bones across the four directions.

As fast as wind the dog flies away from me, calling out at the end of his tones, rolling up and over distant hills that I could not travel in twice the time. I think *mountain lion*, and fear for him, but then I see the brushy flash of coyote tail speeding out, up, and over the rolling hills ahead. Coyote is out for a walk too, an evening hunt, and if opportunity allows, an evening kill. If it wanted, my dog would be no match. But coyote is playing canine games, hide and seek, and the dog has no hope to catch him. He returns, leg- and lung-tired, well satisfied with himself, his tongue lolly-gagging almost to the ground.

The sun approaches the edge of evening—expect a beautiful sunset, one each night—and Hale-Bopp streaming overhead as I make my way back through the Arizona desert to my little cowboy shack on the school campus where I fell in love with my future wife. To all my books and papers, to my cups and clothes, with nothing to feed or tend but myself and the dog and our spirits, flourishing on cool dry air.

Our nature lies in movement; complete calm is death.

PASCAL

V

Whitmore, California, USA—2001

Old Cow Creek is down in the little canyon, a good 500 feet of vertical descent. Walking out across our ten acres, across the dirt road and behind the old Whitmore Cemetery, which my wife and I now own a little corner of, we have cut a passage through the thick manzanita and buckbrush, invading species in this cut-over country.

I make my way out with the dogs, two new dogs now. Kuma went to live and work on ninety-one square miles of open country at the Circle S Ranch in Chino Valley, Arizona. The new dogs are Osa and Lily, sisters from a Queensland mother and a McNab father, lighter in both size and temperament.

Out we go, walking, through the passageway and up and around the old logging roads that got the trucks in and the timber out. The roads are a maze, like the Tokyo subway, and I have taken all the wrong turns before. This time I know where I'm going: out to the bluff's edge and down to the abandoned Gazzigli Ranch.

The road is soft, a cushion of squaw grass and little green sproutings of poison oak. In these parts poison oak can grow twenty, thirty, forty feet up a cedar tree, climbing up through the branches into the canopy. You can't imagine it! But these new shoots in the tread of my path are harmless. They won't survive the passing of feet, day after day. A few other people walk here too, as well as a friend who goes on horseback, a fox that leaves its droppings, looped one over the other, on the tops of stones, skunks, raccoons, deer, some black bears, and even mountain lions pass this way.

We lean into the curve that bends against the cliff face and turns into the sun. I clear fallen limbs and a few stones from the path with short flicks of the end of my walking staff. The broken limbs are airborne a moment, making squirrel sounds in the brush to momentarily alert the dogs. But they are onto something else now, a shock of quail rising from the undergrowth, a turtle's shifting fall from the rock to the water, a frog leaping into the pond. Plop!

The Gazzigli Ranch opens out before us now like green-spring Vermont, the long-waving grasses not yet gone to ugly seeds that stick and bind in my socks and the dogs' fur. And wildflowers blooming here: purple shooting star in bloom across the hill, pink cat's ear, and the blooming buckbrush scented so strong it waters the eyes. The remedy: sweet mint, where the pond meets the shore flowing up along my pants as I pass.

The pond is a long oval with a little rowboat on one side. The old man and old woman Gazzigli died not too many years ago, and their children still own and visit this place. I always know when someone has been here: I see their footprints, the truck tires on the forgotten road; the boat, shifted slightly to the left or to the right. I wonder if they know I have been here, trespassing. I touch nothing. I leave nothing. I travel as light and as fast as I can. Still, I consider, I may not be welcome.

Red-wing black bird calls from the cattails that bend like a bow with the weight of the bird and the breeze. The water surface becomes a reflection of light, driven before itself and shining. Overhead, the great dark shadow is a turkey vulture. Lily, the dog, looks up. She is attracted to birds. That same dark shadow on one occasion was a golden eagle, floating in on nothing, on thin air.

I have never seen a mountain lion, but my wife has, running out behind the old rock quarry up the road a bit. She came into a clearing and watched the amazing length of some creature's thick tail stealing into the underbrush. A little one, a cub. And so, where is mother? The hair came up on the back of her neck, she said, because somewhere deep inside all of us, we know that we are sometimes prey.

The dogs and I descend the steep jeep-scarred path on the hillside: thick clay, easy enough to slip and fall when it rains. I lean on the uphill side of my staff the way my friend Matsui taught me to do in the snow with traditional Ainu snowshoes called kanjiki. On that winter walk in Hokkaido, Mr. Nomoto demonstrated "running down the mountain." He set one foot just before the other, leaned back on the staff like a brake in the snow, and slid all the way down standing straight up. I try it now, remembering that beautiful country, with my Bean boots on slippery California clay; I slide a short distance, get stuck, almost topple over, then slide again and get stuck again, a slide and stick to the bottom, where the patient dogs stand waiting.

I don't enjoy walking so much in the summer heat; the Sacramento Valley smog depresses my spirit. But this time of year everything is so clean and heavenly. I go on through the reedy grasses where the pond pours out into the end of the open space. Oh, give me a cool mossy day, and I'll love God and all gods and the created world! But today I'm wondering if I'll make it through. I'll need something, I say to the crickets and the frogs along the pond, because something must be there for having.

Along the way and through the broken gates out of the cow pasture, I take to the road again. My dogs trot along at a happy clip, drawing their noses down through the long grasses, cupping the blades in their mouths and so tasting the world.

Up there in those stones are two plaques in memory of Mr. and Mrs. Gazzigli, dated with their years of birth and death. I pass them by today.

Storming into my mind are images of a former student I have lost, a girl who graduated from the school where I teach. One year after graduation she was dead, killed in a car wreck on a dark Michigan highway. My wife and I remember her as a beautiful blonde soul, tall and lean and light in spirit. She had a hard childhood, and God knows how or why she became so caring. My wife was especially close to her, and helped her overcome the destructive remnants of an alcoholic father, a half brother who molested her for years, and her mother, a famous opera singer, who would believe none of it, even what she herself had observed.

When the news came in that she had been killed, I found a few poems in my classroom files written in her hand and her old English literature textbook. Inside she had marked a poem with a personal letter from a friend whom she had helped come through a similar past. The poem: "Do Not Go Gentle into That Good Night" by Dylan Thomas. Later I learned that her school counselor said this when he got the news of her death: "I always thought she was too pure, too fragile for this world."

At this place, here at the edge of the pond, my heart falls at the memory of her and the image of her face in my mind, which will fade. The dogs sit beside me now on the bottom of the overturned rowboat. They nuzzle me and ask to be acknowledged. "Here we are!" they tell me with their noses. "Here we are! We are alive!" And to prove it they leap down and scramble tumbling through the long flowers and thick weeds, a whirl of ticks and burrs and life. A light wind sparkles the water pressed soft by the California sun. What can we do except accept the world, its successes and failures, creations and destructions, its living and dying? What can we do, except love this world?

I breathe in the mountain air, and the sun that burns and raves calls in the close of day.

Walk on!

GAUTAMA BUDDHA

Fawn

I was driving Whitmore Road just up from the store, talking with my wife about the house we are buying, this and that, nothing amazing, just before it happened. Two fawns, still dressed down in spots, mother at the extreme side of the road, came so fast out into the track of our coming on that one of them was under the front carriage of the truck before I could hit the brakes. I heard Suzanne say "Oh!" sharply, just too late, and the little deer went whirling out from between the wheels, a trail of exhaust and exhaustion, pitched and yawned across the asphalt, turned over, lay still. And the other, slipping through this slot between life and death, faded into the trees on the other side.

I stopped, our white 1999 Toyota Tacoma at an angle in the road, hesitated, said nothing, and then started forward slowly so as not to be hit from behind by another car. The first feeling I remember is shame, and then double shame for thinking of the truck. I felt ashamed of my wealth, and the distance I was then from the world around me. So decadent in an air-conditioned cab, freshly showered and clothes cleaned and pressed, on my way to Redding to pick up my mountain bike, freshly tuned at the cycling shop, perhaps eat lunch, whatever I wanted, buy a gift for a friend who will complete his third graduate degree next week in Vermont. I might poke around at the bookstore some. Tour rows of new refrigerators, washers and dryers, gas stovetops, all for the new house. Necessities, I called them. So necessary that I, without meaning to (as I reasoned), had exchanged these worldly things for this little life now cooling on the road.

I turned the truck around and went back.

"It's still breathing," Suzanne said before we could park and get out. The fawn had been across the road in Brian Brady's green irrigated hay field. Brian always complained about how much of his livelihood he lost to deer, but even he didn't want it this way.

"What can we do?" Suzanne said, as we approached the wreckage in the road. Nothing, I thought. Nothing at all. But I would at least pull the dying fawn from the roadway. I would at least allow it to die in the shaded trees close to where its twin went in. So close, that edge between making it and not making it. Perhaps, I hoped, such a gesture—and still it was nothing more than a gesture—would offer some kind of redemption.

I gathered the thin hind legs like cut flower stems in my hands, and began to drag the fawn across the road. It kicked, squirmed and pulled away from me. More life here than I expected. So I knelt, and taking the tiny head in my left hand, folded the baby into my arms. It mewed like a kitten, a mournful sound. I carried it across into the cool trees, laid it gently in a bed of squaw grass.

The fawn was breathing fast and warm on my arm, its eyes closed, unconscious. I ran my hands down the length of its legs, across its back, palpating the muscles and bones. Nothing broken, I thought. I found abrasions. Bloody scrapes from the friction with the road. One on the right hind leg. Another small red strawberry on its left side. Across its head, to my shock, most of the hair was torn away. It was scalped and skinned, pockets of pain, and it bled from behind the soft petals of its ears.

This is not the first time for me. I struck and killed a deer on Highway 21 just north of Lowman, Idaho, with a 1989 Ford pickup that wasn't mine. That was ten years ago, and I was all of twenty-one years old. The image of that deer exploding in adrenaline dream-time, hoof and bone and hair, haunts me still. I've killed my share of gray squirrels, nothing to do for them. A jackrabbit on a lone dirt road in central Arizona; the car behind me struck it again. A few snakes, curling in the rearview mirror. A slow tarantula out the Dugas Road. In eastern Oregon on Highway 97 near Shaniko, through a dense frozen fog in January, three bald eagles on a road-killed rabbit came into the sudden space in front of me. Two lifted off and away. The third, as if frozen in fear, stood its ground as I rushed on, and then, just before impact, up and off it flew, thumping into the hood, sliding up onto the windshield in a majestic chaos washing over, still in flight but out of control, and then stable again, wings steady and floating off, dazed and hurt into the winter wind. I sat there on that cold empty highway for I don't know how long.

Suzanne and I are busy buying a house, as I already said, and in the moment of the fawn I felt a deep loss of interest here, a loss of safety, a loss of home. In an instant the world transformed from a place of great excitement and fortune to a place of instability and danger. The day was hot, over 100 degrees Fahrenheit in the valley, and the sun burned holes in my heart.

Oh, we have taken too little care of this. Another death on the road is a deep blow to hope. As Barry Lopez writes in his essay on this same topic, "Who are these animals, their lights gone out? What journeys have fallen apart here?" Not that I, or anyone, may sew these torn fabrics together again, but the very least we may do is take these creatures and their stories into our thoughts and our hearts. I don't mean, let's have pity or gush a sentimental sigh. I mean, let's acknowledge the world and its inhabitants as we pass through it in the pods of our speeding lives. I mean, let's offer some gesture to help restore dignity to creatures flattened on the road. Or, for that matter, for some fellow human being flattened by the weight of his own life. I mean, let's stop and think about that.

The fawn panted, its head in my hands, eyes fluttering. I thought it must have been a severe concussion, and the longer it remained in the between-world of consciousness and unconsciousness, the better chance it had of dying, right then, in my arms. I was quite sure that it would. I moved my thumbs gently in small circles around its mouth and cheeks, and under its ears. I would stay with it to the end, and then carry it deeper into the woods. Not for burial, but simply to lay it to rest where the coyotes and turkey vultures, and eventually the flies, yes the flies, would care for it in their own way. The eyes fluttered open, dim and blank, closed again, and then the fawn woke up, lifted its head and looked around, bewildered, and then softened again, pillowing its face in my palms. What now? It might just make it. Would Suzanne and I drive it home and settle it in for care-taking? Bottle feed it, water and goat's milk? Or would we leave it here and let nature take her course? Let the little fawn live or die according to its strength and to its luck?

A young boy on a bicycle whizzed by on the road. The fawn stood up then, panicking into the sharp blackberry vines. It stood bobbing back and forth on its unsteady legs, its back now turned to me, head thrust through the spiky tendrils. I touched it again. It started, and pushed through the vines into the covert tangle of manzanita and poison oak. It turned back to look at me, a blackberry thorn imbedded in the soft side of its nose. I watched it watching me, still unsteady on its legs and blinking its big eyes. A car passed now on the road again. The fawn's ears turned toward that rough sound.

"We should leave it here," I said. "We should go now."

"Yes," Suzanne said. And then, "Look there." I did. Peering out from the edge of the wood was the tiny twin, the sibling we'd seen make it across the road before our wheels came crashing through. And there we were, still as stones, the two of us, looking at the two of them. That, I felt then, was a gesture. And I exchanged this gesture of hope with these two creatures of the woods.

You know this one by Frost:

Two had seen two, whichever side you spoke from.
"This *must* be all." It was all. Still they stood,
A great wave from it going over them,
As if the earth in one unlooked-for favor
Had made them certain earth returned their love.

The Way to Coss Creek

An ancient Buddha said, "A painting of a rice-cake
does not satisfy hunger."

DOGEN

The way to Coss Creek takes us winding in and out along the contours
of the land. The road leans into the mountain where the creek has
carved its path and back out again, skirting the edge of the mountain,
jutting into the empty space left by the big canyon. Driving this way
together we cannot know in the cover of evening darkness if the tires
will hold to the winter road, if the next turn will curve us out over the
precipice and release our bodies to the wind. It is early evening, just
after four o'clock, but the days are short and the dark storm is bearing
down. Two women in the back seat, talking, me driving, driving the
green car to a hot springs bath.

The local people who know the way to Coss Creek will not accept
my telling you which roads to follow, which turns to take. It is a place
known by too many outsiders already, they would say. They took a great
risk in leading me here the first time. But you see, despite the man-
ner in which they hide themselves to outsiders, they also wish to open
their secret places to people who will care for them, to people who will
touch those places tenderly, like a mother nurses a child. In this way

these places may keep going on. So, you see, we are a kind of hope for them. If you are the right person to hear this story, the forgotten way will reveal itself. This story is for someone who already knows, so that she will remember.

The way to Coss Creek isn't hard to find. Go there. Follow the road leaning into the mountain, the one out to Round Mountain, and then to Big Bend, a little place between other places where no one pauses on their way.

Through town you will come to an old bridge. The transportation department is rebuilding this bridge, and on some afternoons a bold worker might follow a lone woman down to the springs. She has come to soak in the warm Earth water. He has come to search out symbols of divinity. But neither will get what they want with the other around. It's a wonder something else hasn't happened.

You can park anywhere here at the side of the road. If you pull up a little farther, beyond the place the bridge extends out over Coss Creek, up the dirt road there, that is a good place to park. The three of us park here and walk out along the creek, along the dirt path, against the flow of the water, under the cover of darkness. We wear long underwear, warm fleece pullovers, and walking boots in the cool wetness of the night. We talk a little, but mostly we just walk into the cool, wet darkness of the night.

Just a mile or so, maybe less, we come to where the winter creek has swollen across the road bed. We have to go around. Holding onto willow branches thin and cold like white bones, we keep our feet dry this way, walking along the edge of the water and leaning back on the strength of the willow branches, alive and cold and green.

The pathway fans out into a gravel bar, a delta, a little confluence of feeder creek and Coss Creek, all the water coming together. Just over there is the warm Earth water, the hot springs. Why we have come. We walk there.

Now this is new: someone has hauled a fiberglass hot tub out here, mortared it in, directly onto the rocky shore, and drained off enough water to fill it from the hot pool. That old stone pool that fills the fiberglass hot tub is very hot. Almost too hot to sit in, but just right after getting used to it. This new fiberglass pool is just a bit cooler than that, so it's easy to get into right away.

We set our bags down on the wet rocks.

It has been raining and snowing here for three days, and everything looks wet and shining. The stars, occluded by the speeding night clouds, are visible in and out of moments. A moon brightens the foggy air, a quiet penumbra. We undress, not speaking at all. We lay our clothes in careful piles up under the cover of cedar and Douglas fir. It is going to rain again.

She is first, naked and slender in her legs and waist and shoulders and heavy in her chest, turning and smiling and bending to steady herself going into the bath, into the gentle rocking of her breasts and nipples, hardened in the sensual sloping of her breasts, warmed and sensual in the beauty of being naked in the open world. And she is next, slipping in behind, her shape womanly and vital, into the triangle of her pubis slipped under and the shape of her delicate eyes and nose, her hair long and dark and grayed and wet at the bottom where she slides in, closes her eyes against the moment, and holds her breath a moment more before she exhales and the weight of heavy things falls away and washes over the sides of the deep Earth pool with the water in the shape of the space that she is in the world. And I am after that, naked and male and slipping in across from them both, our bare feet touching in threes.

The water pools around us; the quiet pools around us; the dark pools around us. The white snow falls out of god's sky.

Nothing happens for a long time.

Then she digs into the bag we have packed along. She opens a plastic container of red wine poured out of the glass bottle for carrying, offers it to me beside her, and we trade it across ourselves, tipping it back in turns and sharing the edge of it with our lips.

She opens a container then, and holds it for each of us, her hands holding it, passing it around, and like Romans we dine on grapes and hard parmesan cheese, a few crackers and grapes, more cheese, until all of it is gone.

Feeling light now with the wine and the hot water and the company, we move from pool to pool, hot pool to just a little cooler pool; we sit out on the cold rocks, naked and shining and bold in the winter air. The snow stings our hot skin, and mists away. We talk and don't talk, laugh and don't laugh, touch and don't touch, eat and drink and don't eat and drink under god's sky.

Something else is in the air, in the mood of being what we are where we are. Our feet touch around the rock and each other as our hands had around the food and the wine we passed until it was empty. That passed too. And the moon fell out of sight.

Darker now, we each find our naked way to our clothes, keep our eyes to ourselves, mostly to ourselves, slip things on over our talking and touching and eating and drinking and laughing smooth bodies, buckles and buttons and belts, buckled and buttoned and belted on. We load up the bag and walk out the way the water goes down Coss Creek, the way the water goes that is Coss Creek, the thing itself, nothing separating anything now, together, for this moment, not even the dark.

Maybe it is the light that separates us, the fear of it, of what might be seen. We walk this way, knowing the light will come, side by side, remembering ourselves and each other's bodies, and holding on to the warm freedom of the clean Earth.

Letter to a Young Girl at Summer's End

L ight falls away with the seasons and its leaves into this time at summer's end where it has not rained in many, many weeks. Temperatures reach 108 degrees in the valley, day after day, and the river swells unnaturally because politicians release water from the reservoir for irrigation downstream. The California black oaks without water have too early gone yellow, the poison oak is turning red, and blackberries, late this year, are meager and tart. Even the black bear, who is not usually selective, has turned away to other endeavors. North of here, the season's first wildfire burns at twelve hundred acres, and spreading. Friends have been evacuated from their homes, and they go, despite standing strong at first with chain saw, shovel, and garden hose.

I am sorry you had to die. I think of it now, weeks later, your closed casket at the funeral, the garland arranged over the center so that it looked more like a table than a box to lay you in. Forgive me, but I didn't notice at first. I was trying to avoid people I knew, people you

Some phrases in this essay, especially in the final paragraph, rely heavily on Dylan Thomas's poem "Fern Hill."

knew, because I was very tender, and didn't want to cry. So I scanned the front of the church, watched the minister, what he was doing, the woman at the organ (did she know you? or does she do this kind of thing for a living?), the weird little man from the mortuary (why are they always like that?), and then I realized the presence in front of me with the flowers was you.

When your brother came into the church (kind of you to call him that, but you didn't have the same mother), I experienced the truth in everything you said. He was piqued, sharp-nosed, smiling all the time. I could see it in his pasty complexion, his crawling hands, the haggardness about his eyes that he had to bear it, so heavy, for so long. I could see that he still wasn't quite sure if he was safe from what you might say because now, to his surprise, he was burning to say it himself. He rushed in beside your grandfather, who wept old tears, because for him death is very real. Your brother held your grandfather tight about the shoulders, kissed his cheek, spoke to him in his ear. I grew angry. Liar! I wanted to say, but kept my place, because I had never met either of them; I knew them only in your stories.

Remember when we first met? My wife took a job at the boarding school you attended. Before I began teaching there I served as a guest reader for your English teacher. I read a story I had written about my father, and you raised your hand and praised me, said it made you think about your relationship with your own father. You inspired me then, gave me confidence. Later, at home, walking through the alien trees, I thought, *No, wait, that is my job.* But this is the way you were. So selfless. So giving. Freely, as if you didn't know wealth is something people go to war about.

By late August I'm ready for fall, but here summer presses on into mid-October, though we'll have shifts to remind us that winter will come. It's about this time that people begin to realize, again, that the wildfire season is just beginning. I walk outside after the TV news: fires burning in six western states. The trees on my land are calling out for water. The ground is soft and brittle, fine, like powdered sugar. I close my eyes and wish for the end of clear skies, tomatoes hot on the vine, and the evening sounds of crickets when the heat rises out of the day. But perhaps one should not hope for fall too soon.

Your mother came into the church, supported by one of the pallbearers and quivering in her bottom lip. I'm sorry, but that was an act. She was wearing her opera face, the one she knows best from so many years on stage: one-fourth joy, three-fourths sorrow. Her hair was swept up and back, loose, but stabled by something styling it. She wore makeup, but you couldn't really see it. She wore a long silk scarf that flowed up around her face and a dress that was both comfortable and sensual. She made a beautifully sad face all the way to the back of the church, and then sat down. She was all right after that; she rested her character a little. She loves you. She is deeply troubled and broken by your death. But her real feelings have been too long tangled with Desdemona, Zerlina, and Susanna, and it isn't your fault she hasn't said what she wants to say.

Your father? He is a big, fragile man. You have seen this all your life, I know. His tears come out dry, soaked in alcohol. He thanked me for coming, my wife especially, for talking at the service about how honestly you lived at the school. And then she read your favorite poem.

In the fall of 1988 a fire came through Montgomery Creek, just thirty miles or so from my house. I didn't live here at that time. It started near a spring at the crest of the grade. Years ago the town built a drinking fountain here, because on a hot summer day it was a godsend to both driver and radiator. It's a funny thing, a stone fountain with a spigot way out on that empty highway hill. But the world isn't as safe as it used to be and you can't drink that water anymore. That's where the fire started.

The way I heard it, someone dropped a hot cigarette, filled a milk jug for an overheating Chrysler, and sped away. The cowboy at the top of the hill across the highway watched the wind whip the fire up and carry it over the road. It rode up the steep slope onto his property. The first fire crew arrived from the California Department of Forestry ("CDF" to folks around here). From the back of his house the cowboy could see the big red engine down there, idling, waiting for orders. He called out on the two-way radio in his pickup truck. "Hey," he said, "I need some help up here." The engine responded that they were waiting for orders. The cowboy knew that he was alone. He set up the lawn sprinklers on the roof and then began to halter his horses one by one. By that time the fire was rolling through the trees next to the house. He couldn't see through the smoke eclipsing the sun, or even hear from the roar of the fire exploding into the trees. The horses were panicked and gasping and flashing into the dark; one went down from so much smoke as he steadied it to buckle the halter. He left it lay. He got the halter fastened this time onto a big roan, and leading it toward the trailer, its legs unsteady, it leaned into him as he tried to pull it by the lead rope, and then to push it from the side into the trailer as its legs buckled, weighed over onto him in a slow, arcing roll, pinning him there against the firm Earth. He couldn't move. He thought he was dead.

The fire broke loose over the property, burned and raged, consumed the house and the barn and ripped through the horses lying side-long and smoke dead. The one on top of him saved his life. The fire ran up over the hill, and he crawled out from under with only a broken shoulder and a few minor burns on his face and hands.

Before that it was all tall timber as far as you could see. Now, fourteen years later, yes, it has all been replanted. But when you drive through it's still nothing, a few new houses in a sea of charred poles and stunted green trees. Most of those people didn't have the strength to rebuild. We call it the Fountain Fire, and for some it's still burning.

After I heard you were killed, I went to my classroom, alone. I knew your textbook was among the stacks to be resold to new students in the fall. So I dug it out, and leafed through the pages and the class notes in the margins written in your hand. When I found you had marked the poem that way, I couldn't keep my own tears back to see the words. The note you left there in the pages was from another student who so deeply trusted you, loved you, praised you for helping her in hard times. And the Dylan Thomas poem. Here are the words now, the part I remember best about how you worked to live:

Curse, bless, me now with your fierce tears, I pray.
Do not go gentle into that good night.
Rage, rage against the dying of the light.

It was a violent wreck, I know. The newspapers described everything, how the car topped 70 miles per hour in that ritzy neighborhood, ramped the curb and plowed up trees along the manicured walkway. The three of you who died, as the doors came off in the leaves, flew out like birds from the nest, far out beyond gravity and into the welcoming darkness of the expanding sky. Perhaps you felt released (at last) from the pressure of being young and beautiful, from the car and the aggression of the driver inside who had insisted he wasn't drunk and how dare you and forced you in. Perhaps you felt released from your family, from your body, from the solid Earth that held you down, and maybe, in that final moment you felt a deep desire to live, and deep regret too, because if only you hadn't been in that car, if only you hadn't been drinking, if only you had stayed home, if only you had been born into a different time, if only . . . But you were too far outside the world already, and you parted from us, from yourself there in the hurling dawn, and when what was left came down it was not you anymore, but a broken shell that grounded everyone you ever touched.

This boy who was driving? He had cut the seat belts out of the back seat? I can't understand that. He was saved by the airbag? And when the car stopped, he ran off into the rows of cookie cutter houses. Eight hours later he showed up at the city police station with his parents and a lawyer. I also heard that the other boy who lived crawled from body to body to make sure no one was alone, and he settled your summer dress down over you and passed out with his finger at your pulse that had already gone still. But what I think about most is how lonely you must have felt.

You know, not long after all this, one of the teachers at school lost his rented house to a fire. He was young, my age, and he had driven into town with a friend. I don't know how it started but the helicopters came in over the trees like pelicans sailing the troughs and peaks of waves, and bombed the place with water, showering his meager holdings, his books and bike and bed, as the fire raged green as grass. Did you know that I lived in that same house less than a year before?

Understand that your little sister will struggle with guilt forever. She wanted to be you. To her you are perfect, especially now. The truth of it is clear in your physical differences. She is terribly overweight. Of all the avenues to tell the world about her pain, she would have chosen yours. But you got to it first. All that she had left was to be your opposite. Somewhere inside she always wanted you to die. Now she wishes it had been her instead.

Do you know what your counselor at the school said? When he heard about the accident? He said he always thought you were too pure for this world.

Summer is at its end now. We have not had any rain. Every day the sky is blue and fires rise up in the mountains to the west. The smoke settling in over the river valley is hard on the lungs and the spirit. The leafy trees are saying so, turning their colors, green and dying, and letting fall their leaves. "Too soon, too soon," we all say. And we all say good-bye to you, the sky gathering again, green and golden, spinning, spellbound, a wanderer white under the simple stars. You, walking on, to the fields of praise.

A Horse Builds a Woman in a Storm (A Dream)

She moved barefoot among the horses in the summer night, their nervous hooves drumming the dry ground. She trailed her sun-stained hands over their withers, down their angled backs, into their soft, spreading flanks. The slow motion of her hands steadied their flared blowing as she made her way to each animal, settling it with her hands as its settling settled her.

She found Brownhorse among them, a thoroughbred with a racing history under the name Jackpot Luck, and put her hands out for him, easing him away from the crowding ranch horses. He reached for her with his soft mouth, for what she might have for him, searching the air with his horse lips like hands. Brownhorse. Brownhorse. She called his name softly. Brownhorse. He always came to her when she called his name. Always.

She knew the place on his broad rump that captured him. She scratched him there with the tips of her fingers. He stood still for her, one hind leg cocked, the other bent loose, hung there like a broken screen door. She felt the oil of his skin in her fingers, the hair coming loose that would come loose and the sloughing of dry skin. His lips curled in opposite directions, almost twisted ecstasy over themselves. His teeth just visible, white, his neck stretched like a giraffe's. His eyes closed half, fluttered open, half-closed.

This is how she made it safe for him. This is how she expressed her love.

She gathered her loose summer dress into a knot at her left hip and took a handful of mane. Brown mane. She swung up high with her right leg, her female center now against the warm, live animal.

She pushed her woman's gentles down the sharp spine of Brownhorse until her hips rested over his, her spine followed along his, her head to one side of his, her arms loose around his round ribs. She lay there for a moment, a moment, and then let out all her breath. She closed her eyes. Big soft eyes. Blue eyes. She closed them. She would let Brownhorse take her where horses went in the night.

The husband lay asleep in the house. He had not heard his wife get up and go outside. The dogs chirping at the kitchen door to follow her. The gate opening and closing. The horses moving nervously near the barn.

Brownhorse followed the long bow of the fence, railroad tie posts bound by long sun-worn two-by-sixes. The moon was there, alight and round. The ranch horses followed behind because ranch horses would follow, travel together, in the night. Always. They all went that way, north into the open country edging the mountains, the mountain peaks visible in the moon's light, if one looked in against the sky for them. Big Bear Mountain. Soft Top. Devil's Finger.

The woman on the back of Brownhorse followed the rhythm of his walking, her shoulders rising and falling with his, her hips rolling over his, her head jarring when his step went long or short. She followed his body, did with her body what he did, let herself go that way so that it felt like floating.

It was nothing new to her to travel with horses this way. When she was a child, when she was an adolescent, when she was in college and trying to love a man, it was the only way she had to settle the shapes in her mind, to ground the sounds of shadows, the wood-creaking of steps on steps up the stairs, something coming in the night, that thing from long ago in her memory. She hugged herself close beneath the blankets. Something stopped at her bedroom door. She hugged herself.

Light cut open the room. She kept hold on herself. Something peering in, peering deep into the room, so long peering in, so deep she could not hide. She wanted to scream. Thieves! she might have screamed. Thieves! the word so loud it rang in her ears. But she did not, and the shadow came inside. This is the way she made it safe for herself: she hugged herself close beneath the blankets. This is the way she expressed her love: she escaped from her body into the rafters. In the morning, when the family gathered for breakfast, she found she could not look at the father's hands.

Brownhorse made his way to the creek. The woman held her eyes closed, but she was aware of the presence of water in the sharp cooling of the night air, in the soft moisture moving over her, in the sound of it, in the sound of the singing frogs. Brownhorse bent to drink. Ranch horses bent to drink all around them. Brownhorse passed his soft mouth over the surface of the pooling water, back and forth in the shape of a Japanese fan. The water came in long draughts so she could hear the water washing through the horse's body, the mountain water cooling him, cooling her. Cleansing him, cleansing her. When Brownhorse lifted his head to listen for something, water ran in long rain lines from his mouth back into the creek and swirled away.

She was the oldest daughter by five years, and felt responsible for her two sisters. She protected them, taking on the blame for everything, for nothing, wrong or right, to absorb the mother's skeletal blows. The fists came fast and empty when they came, the fingers curled like yellow chicken feet. They struck hollow, closing on themselves. There was nothing in those hands, and they made sharp, vacant slapping sounds against her shoulders and arms and inside themselves, clapping together like clams. She could take it, she told herself, because the pain was not in her. This is how she made it safe for them: she would take the blows for her sisters. This is how she expressed her love: she would absorb the mother's pain, all of it, whatever it was, however much it was.

Brownhorse moved through the tall grasses along the creek edge, far beyond the house and barn. The woman could not taste the grass he bent for, but she knew the green smell of grass cut by horse teeth, the rhythmic chewing, the sharp pauses that came with sharp night noises, the slow motion grazing forward over the old grass to the new grass. The water sounds, bleeding water sounds, pouring off the country in the night. These were patterns she knew. These were sounds she knew. This is how she made it safe for herself. This is how she expressed her love. A pattern of clouds built against the mountains, a gathering of forces in the sky.

Up in the house the husband slept soundly. He spread out into the place his wife had been, something of her still there. He didn't notice.

He wanted to understand it, and so she would tell him how it had been, how it was for her now. She would say that she wanted something solid beneath her, call it "what she needed from him." And he would say, all right, he would try to do that, he would try to be that. But in practice he didn't understand. They came to this place, this conversation, over and over until they exhausted themselves and could not be near each other for a time. And they talked often about letting the other go.

Light split open the night, headlights from a pickup truck ahead at the end of the pasture. Who was it? Who was coming? A blade of light across the grass startled the horses. She heard voices. Two? Three? She couldn't hear the numbers. Poachers. She didn't want to be seen. Deer in the headlights. She wanted to hide. She hugged herself into Brownhorse as close as she could, a dark hump on a horse's back. Pickup doors opening, closing. She hugged herself close. Laughing, she heard laughing like hot breath and stumbling drunk in the summer. Empty cans clanging in the back of the pickup. It was loud. Shattering loud. No, she said. Her heart racing now, the horses moving together, moving faster, running, their noses flaring as they ran into the light, concealing her. No, she called out, the word as loud as the horses' hooves, hooves thundering like rain. No. The laughing like lightning in her ears. Brownhorse running faster and faster, the other horses trailing (this is the way he made it safe for her), sweeping the corner of the pasture in his speed (this is the way he expressed his love) straight through the cut of light and off into the distance.

The husband woke to find his wife gone. He lay there a moment in her absence, trying to sense how long she had been gone. He swung his legs over the edge of the bed, put his feet on the floor. The floor was cool and hard, the wood cool and hard. The dogs came to him, nervous and pushing their noses into his hands. He stood up. The only light was the moon through the window, enough for him to dress without bothering with the light. He laced up his boots. He put on his hat.

Perhaps, they had told each other, love was not enough.

The woman lay exhausted on the soft back of Brownhorse, walking now toward the barn, still blowing from the speed. A light rain fell over her hot skin. Cool, soft drops. Raindrops. She expected it, but it always surprised her when it came. The horse moved on toward the barn.

When the husband reached the barn in the rain, he saw Brownhorse coming in with the ranch horses and the woman. He walked out to meet them. He took the hand of the woman, who then became his wife again as she came down from the horse. He held her up, cradling her in his arms, and led her out of the rain.

A Matter for Heron

On days of rain along the river, seasons are indistinguishable. You are just as likely to say it is late fall when it is summer, or believe that it is early winter when it is spring. The sky swells and pushes out the edges of the valley-border mountains and you expect the rain to never end and the trees to retain their wet-green and the desert to request that the spotted owl accompany its transformation to temperate rain forest.

Blue heron is advantaged by such days. He comes to the rocky bars along the river and fishes his long ostrich neck into the clouded air, then curls it again upon his blue-gray feathers. He will raise one leg and stand balanced, forming a rain-shed with his back. Water beads and travels down the veins of his feathers.

Blue heron will outstand the length of the rain. When crow and eagle have sought their shelters, he will be there still, listening, the river coming around the one leg, the course, uplifted banner of feathers atop his head matted and directing rain. The eyes seemingly never sleep.

When blue heron moves, it is never sudden. He will turn his head in frames from east to each direction, evaluate his posture and crank his neck in time with his legs as he goes. He will not move far before settling his feet among the rocks again and lifting the reptilian age of his leg. Blue heron cares not that he is cousin to the alligator and the snapping box turtle. He cares only for rain.

To pressure blue heron into flight is no simple task. Thunder does not stir him into the air. He is solaced by that booming music, for when he hears it, rain is almost certain to follow. He does not care for passing geese or common merganser. He pays no more attention to them than he does to a sudden flash of electricity across the sky. To move blue heron requires the voices of people, the slipping-by of a canoe.

And when you see blue heron crouch and push upward with his neck and shoulders you will know you have missed it. One moment he is dark and as quiet as stone, the next low, lengthened, and hanging just above the river, his spindled mounts dropping then tucking beneath him. You will believe you are about to fly with him. But he is high now, following the shapes of trees, and you are released from this meditation by the outline of distant wings.

Now each time the sky grays with rain you will be inclined to leave whatever you are doing to search out the location of blue heron. He will be there in the rain just above the place you found him last. And when he lifts and stretches across open space you will wonder where it was he was before the rain—if he was always there.

The Rescue

The doctor said, "Get him out of there." The associate headmaster, who just happened to be my wife, said, "We have to get him out of there, and you are the only one who can do it." Which of course wasn't true, but it felt exciting to think so, that I was the only man capable enough for the job.

I was teaching senior English at a private mountain high school in northern California for the troubled children of the overly moneyed. By "troubled" I mean that these young men and women secreted away a lot of pain from their private tragedies, tragedies that mostly centered on family relationships: the death of a parent; parents who were so busy making money they hired a nanny to do the parenting, which is a kind of death; adoption, the ultimate rejection and abandonment; physical and sexual abuse, sometimes by a parent, sometimes by a sibling; divorce; struggles with sexual identity, which was mostly a problem when it violated the family ideal. The drug use and prostitution (mostly among girls, but not always) were not necessarily the problem, but rather symptoms of these deeper wounds.

Every summer I led backpacking trips as part of our wilderness program, a program that insisted that a balance of community and solitude against the blank slate of nature would help to move these young people beyond their private dramas and at the same time foster a personal environmental ethic. I had grown up in rural Oregon and spent my boyhood romping through the wild Cascades. I seemed to have turned out all right, so mostly I believed in the school's philosophy of the healing power of nature. But I was also a bit of a skeptic. Easy to feel holy when you're out in the woods and scared to death of things that go bump in the night, but upon reentry into the seduction of American voluptuousness I held little hope for most of them. They proved time and again, that after completing the two-year program at the school, they mostly picked up where they had left off.

At any rate, when the associate headmaster, Suzanne, my wife, asked me to fetch the boy, to bring him back to the school campus from the ten-day backpacking trip on the Lost Coast, I accepted as if embarking on a knight's errand.

You see, he had injured himself in a private way. To be more clear, he had injured his private self, in a private way, in a circle of boys all trying to injure their private selves, because, frankly, they had decided to believe that a pierced member, a Prince Albert, as it is known, would make them all members of a very special class of young men. It would imbue them with a heroic identity. It was, they insisted, irresistible to women.

That term, "Prince Albert," in case you didn't know, honors the real Prince Albert, the consort of England's Queen Victoria. Crowned in 1837, the queen is credited with leading the way for Earth-shaking advancements in science, medicine, commerce, the arts, indeed the entire Industrial Revolution, during which England was the world's greatest workshop. Shall we also credit her with inspiring Albert to pierce his penis? He did so, or so the story goes. Known as a "dressing ring" during his day, the fashionable piercing was designed to lash the member against the leg so as to minimize the bulge when wearing the very comely, tight trousers of the day. The ring is drawn through the frenulum and out the urethra. Not sideways, but on the bottom of the penis near the head (the frenulum), and then up and out the opening at the tip (the urethra). If this doesn't give you a picture, find one on the Internet. The prince, it is also said, wore his dressing ring to pull back his foreskin for cleanliness and so to keep his member sweet-smelling for the pleasure of the queen. If a Prince Albert would indeed please a queen, perhaps these school boys were onto something? Or, better said, perhaps something had gotten into them?

Let's be playful. The way I heard the story later, these boys sat 'round in a circle, a kind of sewing circle you might call it, with its ring leader, the one boy I was sent to fetch back (let's call him Richard! You can imagine the jokes when the teachers and counselors found out). They sat 'round together with needle and thread in one hand, something else in the other, and raising the vorpal blade head-high—do you see the picture?—counting off to three, a band of brothers, one for all and all for one, two, three! And together they jammed the prick home.

The very next day Richard left for the Lost Coast with twelve other boys from the boarding school, all innocents, and two trip leaders. No one knew about Richard's Prince Albert.

Back on campus, the other boys woke to a new sun, stretched and yawned, and remembered. They inspected their work. A botched job for most of them, the shriveled puppy red and swollen. No one had made it all the way through, except Richard, so they thought. Then these boys, these brave warriors, came forward, terrified that nothing would ever come forward for them again. They showed the school nurse. "Look what we did to ours," they said. "And Richard is out on the trip. We're really worried about his." They were good, loyal boys who cared very much about each other.

"He's still got the thread drawn through it," one of them said.

The nurse felt unprepared for this kind of thing, so she called the doctor. The doctor said what he said, the associate headmaster said what she said, and I loaded my pack for the road.

I traveled six hours west, over the coast range, in a school van with a fat driver who talked mostly about beef, french fries, and God, those beautiful subjects woven and then tangled up so that when I landed on the beach at Black Sands, I was certain that God, like so many teenage boys, had got his start working the grill at McDonald's. I said so long, shouldered my pack, and made my way north up the beach, the mother ocean settling me out, the soft shine of the evening sun mirrored in the great waters.

I had talked with the trip leader, Ken Ferris, via satellite phone before I left campus, and so knew the party was camped at Miller Flat, about nine miles out. I aimed to walk as far as I could in the cover of night, and then find a quiet corner to lay out my bag. I thought I might make it to Gitchell Creek, where beyond lay five miles of beach impassable at high tide. To beat it I would rise at low tide (about 3:00 a.m.), walk in to Miller Flat, and take Richard out before the tide crested again near high noon. The driver would be waiting. If I didn't make it I'd have to wait through another twelve-hour tide cycle and hike out with Richard in the dark.

The first miles were easy, cool and softly light. My steps slipped back a bit in the sand, so I angled down nearer the pulsing surf. At the edge of the watery horizon, I watched the sun softly falling like a bright eye and the moon softly rising like a bright thought along a long line of pelicans drawn up beside me, skirting the waves, their wings moving in concert over the waters.

I thought about bears. I couldn't help myself. The BLM was reporting that black bears were particularly aggressive this year, so all parties were required to pack food in bear-proof canisters. A simple solution: no accessible food = no bothersome bears. I didn't have much food, but not much is still enough, and in my hurried departure I forgot my bear can. Walking alone on the edge of the continent at night under the mystery of god's sky, I was bear bait, and every storm-beached stump ahead of me became a bear until I drew close enough for it to become a stump again.

Rattlesnakes, too. Lots of them this year, the BLM said, right down on the beach, especially active at night! Walking quietly and fast in the failing light, every line of kelp was a snake until every snake was a line of kelp, and I crossed over one, a rattlesnake! It recoiled, hesitated, and then wound away into the dark. I knew I had seen it too late. It could have, if it had wanted to. But it didn't. I walked on.

Overhead, bats scored the night sky, and underfoot, the forgotten husks of sea urchin, trundled and drawn apart under the force of the many boots gone before. An occasional crab shell, so perfect in the shape of the thing that was. Walking out this way I thought of this moment, this now, this holy now, the very thing itself. I said, "My god, just think of it," aloud to the place, the beauty of these elements converging into this story: the bears, the pelicans, the urchin and crab, rattlesnakes, bats in the night, night itself!, high tide and low tide, being alone, tromping out along the edge of it, the long line of the horizon moving north along the continent, and the mangled penis ahead to be extracted with the boy who carried it. What bliss! What utter bliss. "The utmost measure of what bliss / Human desires can seek or apprehend," as Milton put it.

I came up on Gitchell Creek. I heard it murmuring across the sand in the darkness. I dropped my pack near a great log carried in on some great storm, laid out my bag on the sands, and went to sleep.

The centerpiece of the backpacking trip every summer is the solo experience. This particular summer we trip leaders selected the Lost Coast as our destination, that twenty-four-mile stretch of wild California beach running along the Pacific at the foot of the King Range south of Arcata. We had decided that sitting alone for three days with the great mirror of the ocean would do our young people good. Who could not let his ego dissolve a little, facing the vast and deep blue sea?

We separated the genders. The girls went out with women leaders; the boys went out with men, because, as Robert Bly writes in *Iron John: A Book about Men*, the ancient societies "believed that a boy becomes a man only through ritual and effort—only through the 'active intervention of the older men.'" He asserts that "Women can change the embryo to a boy, but only men can change the boy to a man . . . boys need a second birth, this time a birth from men." Likewise, we held, girls needed a second birth, too, a birth into womanhood, better enacted by women.

The solo experience is the ritual and the effort Bly writes about. Two days out on the Lost Coast, the leaders select sites for the boys. Early in the morning each loads a pack with a tarp for shelter from the sun and rain, a pad and a sleeping bag, clothes, a goodly supply of water (a gallon for each day), and one pound of GORP (the only food they will be allowed for the entire experience). We send them out with a journal, and a few writing assignments. Perhaps we ask them to write about their relationship with their parents. Perhaps we ask them to write about choices they've made in their lives that they regret. Perhaps we ask them to ask the journal, themselves, the sea, what you will, for forgiveness. We may ask that each of them bring back a gift, some object of nature, to give to a friend. Some of these boys have never slept outside before, and two nights alone is a great challenge for them. They will lie in their bags as stiff as boards, listening to the night sounds, the soft patter of mice feet across the sands, the overhead rhythm of an owl waiting, and they will all think they hear something huge in the night. Bigfoot, maybe, or, at the very least, a ravenous bear.

When the boys return from three days of solitude we gather in a circle to talk. The boys talk about the night, the darkness and its fears, their past, the people they love, the people they have hurt. We in the circle listen and acknowledge their success. Each of them has passed this trial of solitude, and so we know them now not as boys, but as men.

At least that is how it's supposed to work, but it's never that easy, never that clean. Trying to carry this sense of manhood into the outer world is nigh impossible, since people out there were not part of the circle and do not recognize the ritual and effort. Upon coming out of the wild, out of the school's program, these boys are treated as if nothing at all has changed for them, and so they often slip back into drug use and violence, struggles with sexual and intellectual identity, overpowering feelings of weakness, even self-loathing and depression. Because some of these boys have been out on solo before, they already know this. They tell the boys who have not been on solo about what they know. Instead of going out into nature for spiritual testing, many of these boys find the solitude conducive to little more than jacking-off for three days under an open sky.

My wrist watch woke me at 3:00 a.m. The tide was as low as it could be, exposing tidal pools humming with life. I packed up my sleeping bag, covered in soft salty dew, and my bedroll, then boiled water for coffee and oatmeal. With my little feast in hand I sat back, for just a few minutes, and enjoyed the morning starshine.

I was having a little solo experience of my own, a little needed solitude. A week from now I'd be at Miller Flat leading my own group of boys, enduring injuries and complaints, arguments and fights, general noise and mayhem. Some good things might happen, too, but after a week of it I always felt spent. I wanted only to return to Suzanne and the quiet of my own home. This morning, and for the next five miles at least, I would have the beach to myself, the tides and the sand, the bears and the snakes, the ocean and the sky. I felt grateful.

I started out. I walked myself into a good mood, and thought of the English travel writer Bruce Chatwin, who believed that walking is a poetic activity that can cure the world of its ills. I quite agreed! All the politics and papers of school life fell away and I listened for my steps in the sand as I walked out a happy rhythm. Soon my thoughts turned toward the group ahead. Later this morning they would go out on solo, and Richard wouldn't be with them. So much the better for him. Would he really find "himself" sitting out there on the beach alone? I doubted it. I thought of all the talk therapy these boys endured at the school, three times a week, talking their guts out in a big group with a couple of counselors, whose primary desire was to make them cry. The counselors valued these sessions by the size of the tissue pile on the floor. Am I a skeptic? A party pooper? Passive-aggressive? Whatever. The students at school often talked about the best diversion tactic: whip up some tears during a group session and the counselors don't hammer you so hard the next time. Alas, the backpacking trip was merely an extension of group work. A trick, a disguised cry meeting in the outdoors. Sounded like doo-doo to me, but, as a teacher invested with upholding the program and the school, I would never say so. Still, my true colors prompted me to ask privately: Wouldn't these boys (the girls, too, for that matter) be better off out here under the great sky, not seeking enlightenment on solo, but just being boys?! Walking their too-idle bodies into exhaustion all day, and then coming into camp, setting up, throwing stones into the surf, inspecting creatures in the tide pools, wrestling in the sand, learning how to build a fire, learning how to be friends? In every campus group session I participated in, I wanted to say: "Look! You. Me. Us. Them. We're all little more than a single hair on the universe's great ass! Forget about your little drama and go live your life! Or go die! What else is there?" But I held my tongue.

Despite my cynicism, other questions remained: Where were all these wounded young people coming from? Is this an American phenomenon? Or is this going on in other places? Other countries? And what exactly *is* "going on?" Why are schools like this one needed? These seemed like questions too big to handle on a short morning hike.

Cruising over rocks and sand, I arrived at Miller Flat in good time. Maybe it was 6:00 a.m. I found Ken Ferris's tent, and shook it mightily. "Ken," I said. "Ken. Wake up. I'm here for Richard."

He growled from inside. "Ohhhh. Didn't expect you so early."

"I'm on a mission," I explained.

A biologist and EMT, Ken had already made an initial inspection. "It's really not serious," he said when I asked. "A superficial flesh wound. It's just a scratch. I don't think we need to pull him off the trip."

Which would have been easier for everyone, especially Richard. Word had leaked out, and everyone on campus knew. Not only did he have to face the associate headmaster, the doctor, and his parents, but also his teachers, counselors, and peers. And the girls. Who could say for sure if what he had done was indeed irresistible to them? Not I.

However, staying out on the trip was not an option. Richard had to go, by order of the doctor. His parents, too, wanted him back on campus; his parents who, with his counselor, had worked out some measure of discipline.

I wasn't certain discipline is what Richard needed. Could we blame him for attempting to distinguish himself (however oddly) from other people? Consider: The students who arrive at the school lose all measure of personal freedom and identity. The counseling staff confiscates and stores their clothes, music, makeup, jewelry (which includes all piercings), and anything else, really, that relates to the life they led back home. Their parents must send them new clothes that meet the school's guidelines, which generally means anything from the Land's End catalog. Also consider: The journey itself from home to the school is often an attack on personal freedom. Many of these young people tell nightmarish stories of being picked up by a professional escort in the night. Imagine retreating to your own bed in your own room in your parents' house (the ultimate measure of personal safety) and waking in the darkness to find a large person standing over your bed who says: "Get up. You're coming with me." He might bind your hands if you're not agreeable, and out you go. You get into a car. You get onto a plane. You get into another car and find yourself rising into the mountains of northern California, unsure if anyone in the world knows where you are. Of course, you don't know where you are either. You don't know if you've been kidnapped or if this is your parents' doing, which you suspect but can't imagine. Are your parents sending you away for your own good, or just to get rid of you? Likely both. When asked by a visitor how he came to the school, one of my students retorted, "A three-hundred-pound Samoan."

To me all this seemed partly necessary (it did sound wise to take away drugs and weapons) and partly cruel. The escort part I wasn't sure was even legal. Following these trials, perhaps Richard's attempt to pierce himself wasn't so mad after all. Perhaps he had decided to mark himself as an individual in the only way he had left. I mean, the school couldn't take away his dick, could it?

Ken and I roused Richard from his tent, who then readied his pack while I cooled my feet in the coastal springs. Then we saddled-up and marched out across the misty sands.

But I'm not done with the wound. Self-wounding has a long and storied history. Oedipus, in Sophocles's play by the same name, wounded himself. He gouged out his eyes when he discovered that his whole life had been a lie. It wasn't that he killed his father and slept with his mother—although that might also do it—but rather that he didn't know who he was. He had never really known who he was. For his whole life his eyes had given him a lie, so he took them out. The wound Oedipus gives himself re-enacts the wound his father gave him as a baby. His father pierced his ankles and sent him to his death. Indeed, it is Oedipus's wounded feet that lead him in search of his origin, and in that search he must discover the wound itself and where it comes from. Can you see where this is going? Dennis Patrick Slattery writes in *The Wounded Body* that wounds "always lead to depth and soul, to insight and to a greater weathering of life's events. Wounds also instruct the wounded on a sense of place, time, and belonging, for wounds speak of some form of violation of both self and place."

What everyone enrolled at the school had in common was a wound, and most of these wounds came from parents. I don't know Richard's story, but he came to us wounded, and then he wounded himself. That's not fair, calling him Richard. I want to tell you his real name because this isn't a joke anymore. Only his real name will do, but I don't have his permission, and so I won't. Let me go on a little more. Slattery writes of Oedipus, "Not only does the parent wound him, but the wound eventually parents him. Oedipus becomes most completely himself through the knowledge gained through his old wound." Perhaps the boy's self-wounding was the best thing for him. Perhaps he was unconsciously signaling where and how he needed help. Perhaps you think I'm making too much of this? It's either the boy's wound means something, it is related to his past and will instruct him in his search for "a sense of place, time, and belonging," or it means nothing. You decide.

For my part, looking back on the rescue, I wish I had left him there on the beach that day, left him to go out on solo and care for his wound. I did not rescue him from any danger, as the doctor and his parents had supposed, but I stole him from himself. The wound had been opened by his own hand, and it was only his own hand that could heal it. He needed to face it, not return to the interrogation he would endure on campus.

Years later, I wondered what had become of him? Where did he go after graduating from the school? What is he doing now? Is he still carrying his wound? For me, his story ends here. For him, maybe it goes on.

It was a long hike out for me. By mile fifteen, slipping back in my boots in the sand, my feet burning with wear, the boy drew out a distance between us. He walked with great purpose and dignity, marching out with all his strength. I watched him grow smaller and smaller against the mist rising from the surf. I looked up at the King Range, the tall fir green against the blue sky, then out across the sea. When I looked down the beach again I could see only a faint outline of him in the distance, a little dark thing that didn't seem to be a thing at all. Until, at last, the dark thing slipped away into the future and disappeared.

Banaue Tercet

I

We take a single room at the Sanafe Lodge in Banaue, a tourist town in the Philippine central Cordillera. It's a clean room with two twin beds and splendid views of the ancient rice terraces. I choose one bed for my new wife, Suzanne, and me. My good friend Tony takes the other. The three of us are about the same age, just over or under thirty, which means we're still young enough to be afflicted by stupidity, but old enough to see it coming. We plan to stay for several nights, including New Year's Eve, the greatly anticipated Y2K event at the turn of the millennium.

The proprietor at the Sanafe Lodge is a grumpy woman with short curly hair. She wears a baggy house coat, yellow with bright pink flowers. She's never heard of Y2K. We try to cheer her by taking up a table on the veranda and ordering cup after cup of brewed coffee at an extortionist's price: three cups of coffee equals a room for the night. She goes on frowning. We settle in.

. . .

Travelers come to Banaue to marvel at the amazing rice terraces, engineered and constructed by the Ifugao people. The terraces have been farmed continuously since the time of Christ. They cascade down the rugged mountainsides like stairways from the seat of the gods. The United Nations Educational, Scientific, and Cultural Organization (UNESCO) designated the terraces a world heritage site, and they have been touted as the greatest agricultural achievement in the history of humankind. The tragic news is that a foreign species of worm is threatening the architectural integrity of the terraces and has driven the local people and the scientific community into a panic (although for different reasons). The worm is relatively small—about thirty centimeters in length—but the talk around town is that giant worm-monsters are devouring innocent farmers in the night.

"Why didn't you get us a separate room?" Suzanne asks when Tony steps out. "What if I want to have sex?" She wears her brown, graying hair at shoulder length, slightly curly at the ends, and a tight athletic shirt over her fit body. She used to race road bikes and has legs like pistons. A friend once described her as "classically beautiful." That, and her intelligence and rare confidence, is why I fell in love with her, but as she complains about the room her face morphs into Grendel and she threatens to swallow me whole.

"Just thought we could save some money, that's all," I say. "We're travelers for now, not honeymooners."

"I know what we are. Anyway, I know you didn't want me to come, so don't try to hide it."

"I'm not hiding it," I say. "I didn't want you to come, and I told you so. You insisted. So I thought maybe we could both have what we want."

"Oh yeah, what *do* we want?" Suzanne asks, knowing she won't get the answer she's looking for.

"I told you what I want," I say.

"No you didn't," she says. "You haven't told me. You won't talk about it."

She's right. I don't want to talk about it. *It* is the conversation that never ends. Six months into our marriage, Suzanne announced I had two options: 1) have a baby with her and live happily ever after; 2) don't have a baby with her and she would go have it with someone else. I chose number 2, or, rather, I expected her to choose number 2 when I answered that I wasn't ready for children. But she didn't. She insisted that I hadn't given her an answer. Later, I asked myself why I was sticking around, knowing she was sticking around because she thought she could change my mind.

"You guys ready to go for dinner?" Tony says from outside the door, saving me. He's wearing his characteristic black ankle-high slip-on leather boots with Levis and a short-sleeved shirt. His hair is cut short now, and he no longer wears the earrings that once rimmed his left ear. Tony is intelligent and ballsy, and, at his best, wields a rapier wit. He grew up in Cape Town, South Africa, but we met in Arizona, where he was working on his undergraduate degree and I was teaching English at a private boarding school. Like me, he never stays anywhere for very long, and this, I suppose, is an ailment we both suffer from and a truth around which our friendship blossomed.

"Yeah," I say back to him. "I'm ready. Are you ready?" I ask Suzanne.

"I'm not finished yet," she says, showing her sharp teeth.

"I know, but can't we finish later?" I say. Of course, I'm offering a diversion. "How about we go for dinner? We can talk later tonight."

"Yes," she says frowning. "Let's go. This conversation never ends anyway."

How do you tell your best friend that you don't love him? You do love him, but this is the kind of love that passes between brothers, and your best friend has fallen in love with you in another way. You've already told him that you're not interested, that you only go the one way, but that you don't want to lose his friendship. It isn't personal, you say. You're not rejecting him, it's just that you don't have any desire to sleep with a man.

So then what happens? Your best friend is offended, of course, embarrassed, and he avoids you as much as possible for months, until slowly, slowly, you rebuild a friendship based on a mutual regard for literature and writing, for good food and beer, for adventuring in foreign lands. Question: after your wedding (in which this best friend serves as one of your groomsmen), do you visit your best friend in the Philippines, where he is working with farmers near Mayon Volcano for the Volunteer Service Organization (VSO)? He has been there three years

54   Banaue Tercet

now, and you wish to keep the friendship alive while taking advantage of the opportunity to tour yet another country on your planetary list. Do you take this chance?

Of course you do.

Do you take your wife with you when she insists?

Well, yes you do.

What I wanted most from the trip was a break from the constant fighting with Suzanne, and Tony's counsel to help me cope with the total annihilation of my dream of marital bliss. Suzanne and I were two years into it, and it wasn't going well at all. I thought marriage would include some domestic strife, but that reconciliation would follow, leading us to a deeper intimacy. As it turned out, we were really good at strife but awful at reconciliation. I suppose we were fighting about the three things most couples fight about: children (she wanted them; I didn't), money (we couldn't seem to share), and careers (would we follow her career as a school administrator or mine as a teacher and writer? Our jobs should have gone well together, but when it came to moving up and on, one of us always wound up starting over).

I wanted to travel alone. At first Suzanne encouraged it, thinking it might help us in our differences. "Do something for yourself," she had said. Later she didn't encourage it. "Go alone if you want to, but I'm not going to make it easy for you." She accused me of being gay and wanting Tony more than her. "Why else won't you fuck me?" she had said.

I caved in, and we made the trip together. Now we were both paying for it, and we were about to make Tony pay for it, too.

The three of us go out for supper at the People's Restaurant, and order San Miguel beers with our chicken adobo, a national standard: chicken (or pork or squid) cooked with vinegar, pepper, salt, and garlic. I sit next to Tony and across from Suzanne. After a couple bottles, I'm feeling happy. I don't care about the obvious tension at the table anymore, and when the food comes it tastes great. Tony flirts with the waiter, a young man-boy who is visibly flustered. He seems to invite Tony's advances, but at the same time he's not sure how to respond. Tony speaks excellent Bicol, the local language used near Mayon, and so-so Tagalog, the national language of the Philippines. Tony asks in Tagalog if the man-boy speaks Bicol, and the man-boy shakes his head. He speaks something else, whatever is local to these highlands, and a little English, he notes, for the tourists. "Hello," he says. "I am fine. And you? May I take your order?" He'd like to flirt more, but the restaurant is busy, and he has to get back to work. Tony orders more beers, and the delicate waiter goes to get them.

"You think the wholefuckingworld will come crashing down tomorrow, on New Year's Eve?" I say, a little hopeful.

"Are you crazy?" Tony says. "Nothing will happen. I'd never even heard that term until you told me. What is it: Y-special-K?"

"Y2K," I say. "We almost stayed home, you know."

"*You* almost stayed home," Suzanne says.

"Yeah, I know," Tony says. "But you're not that paranoid."

"Yes he is," Suzanne says.

"You know the State Department issued a travelers' warning," I say, trying to redeem myself. "And every major airline in the world has canceled flights on New Year's? So I'm not the only one."

"Yeah, I heard," Tony says. "But even if every computer in the world crashes, no one in Banaue will know about it. Things will carry on here as always." He pauses, then smiles. "Of course, we will be carrying on here, too."

"That's comforting," I say.

"What shall we do tomorrow?" Suzanne says.

"Anything you want," Tony says.

Tony and Suzanne have known each other longer than I have known either of them. In fact, before I came along they enjoyed a steamy romance that lasted at least a couple of weeks. I didn't hear about it until after Tony and I were best friends and Suzanne and I were unhappily involved. It occurred to me that we make a weird love triangle, and the only side unconsecrated is the one between Tony and me.

"I think we should make a long hike through the terraces," Suzanne announces. "I really need to get outside. That bus ride sucked."

She means the all-night journey to Banaue from Puerto Gallera, where the three of us had enjoyed several days on the beautiful Sibuyan Sea. "Enjoyed" is relative here. We enjoyed the sun and the water and the beer, but Suzanne and I were hardly speaking to one another and Tony ran interference. After all that relaxation, just imagine eight hours on a forty-foot bus stuffed with people, their luggage choking the aisle, the air conditioner on so high we had to bundle up, passing huge cargo trucks on blind corners at night on a precipitous mountain road headed downhill over a bridge. If you had to attach an adjective, I suppose "sucked" is the one that worked.

"We'd have to hire a guide," Tony says. "It's too much trouble."

"No, it's not. Let's do it," Suzanne says. "I really need to get outside."

She's an athlete, and goes mad if she doesn't get exercise. Tony is a bi intellectual with an overactive libido, and that's the only exercise he's interested in. Maybe I'm somewhere in between.

"I wouldn't mind some time just with you," Tony says to me.

"That would be good," I say.

Suzanne shows her sharp teeth again through her fake smile, then looks out the window into her reflection.

"Yeah," Tony says. "I've got a lot to tell you about."

Suzanne and I talked about this before we left California. She agreed, even encouraged me to hang out with Tony, just the two of us, at least once during the visit. After weaseling in on the trip, she wanted to be open and trusting. I sent this message ahead to Tony, and he and I confirmed, yes, we'd spend an afternoon together, brother to brother. But now, at the suggestion of it, Suzanne is visibly irked; perhaps this isn't the time.

"How about we plan that for the day after?" I say. "Tomorrow let's hike up to Batad."

This seems like a good compromise to me; both Suzanne and Tony will get what they want within twenty-four hours, and also during this time the calendar will turn over to the year 2000. The world will either go on as always or be totally annihilated.

"Yeah," Tony says. "Then we'll have time to talk the day after."

"Good," Suzanne says, "I think I'll go mad if I don't get outside."

We all go back to the room after dinner and sleep uncomfortably in the two beds. I lay next to Suzanne, stiff as a board. She's curled away from me and against the wall. I can hear Tony's deep breathing, the sign of unencumbered sleep. I stare into the darkness, the only window in the room softly aglow with the lights of the town. I wish that I were alone.

From Banaue, the village of Batad is about sixteen kilometers east out along a rutted dirt road then a two-hour hike up over the summit. My guidebook announces it as one of the most beautiful villages in the central Cordillera, a must-see spot for travelers.

We hire a tricycle (a little motorcycle taxi with room for two, but somehow we convince the driver to take all three of us) and speed through town on our way out. The driver curses and slows as he negotiates the cavernous potholes in the road. The motor curses, too, belching black smoke as we pull alongside another tricycle and rocket around. On we fly, down the dirt road, dodging chickens, dogs, children, and jeepneys loaded with people, those retrofitted jeeps left behind after World War II and now indispensable as public transport. At the road's edge a steep green canyon drops hundreds of feet to a frothing river. Jagged emerald peaks tangled in the mist tower over us. We approach a gap where the road has partly washed away. Without hesitation, the driver accelerates into the turn.

By the time we arrive at the trailhead my wits are frazzled. A long climb to the summit and a steep descent into the valley sounds like torture to me right now. I find myself wishing I had opted for a day in town with Tony. But too late. We pay the driver and start walking.

The first half-hour is easy and the trail uncrowded. We ascend into the mountain heights without talking, just walking happily in the quiet through the verdant trees mostly absent of birdsong.

The Philippines is native to some impressive creatures. Of particular note is the mouse deer, the smallest deer in the world. To counter it, the Philippine eagle, sometimes called the monkey-eating eagle, is the largest eagle in the world. Then there is the tarsier, which is the smallest primate in the world, and also the sinarapan, the smallest edible fish in the world. It seems this island nation does nothing in the middle. Yet all of these creatures are endemic to other parts of the Philippines, and all we see on the trail to Batad, besides an attractive couple from Israel, is the occasional domestic water buffalo, known as the "farmer's friend" because they pull everything from plows to wagons without complaint.

The day warms up—it's winter, but we're in the tropics—and we sweat our way to the summit. Young boys are selling cold soda pop and shouting at us in English. They're all about the same size, and naked but for their shorts. "Hey Joe!" they call out, meaning G.I. Joe, another carry-over from the war. "Hey Joe! Cold drink?" They've taken particular pains to hump ice up the mountain from town, but we decline, and linger over the long vista. A sign asks us to "help Batad maintain beauty and traditional landscape through controlled development," then pronounces that we are looking at an "engineering marvel," a "rare man-made landscape" due to the "amphitheater-like form and almost vertical terraced ponds." Indeed, the green terraced hillsides are beautiful and marvelous. The Israeli couple reaches the top and starts down the other side without pause. We're ready, too, and follow them.

We descend into the valley through a forest of pines for which this part of the Philippines is famous. The village below invites us, a tidy arrangement of traditional Ifugao houses on stilts, some with the centuries-old style thatched roof, others with newer tin roofs. The trail leads us directly into someone's backyard, and a small boy leaps out of the jungle and cuts us off.

"You need guide? I take you waterfall," he says.

He's wearing flip-flops and shorts, nothing else. He looks fit and healthy, probably doing a good business preying on stupid tourists like us. We know there is a waterfall down here, the famed Tapplya waterfall, but we don't intend to try to find it. I've seen hundreds of stretches of water coming off rock in different places in the world. They all looked generally the same. Or am I missing something? Seems to me the waterfall is merely a point of focus, a locale to give wanderers direction. Or perhaps another pretty scene to convince travelers that they got something for their effort and money. At least on this day, I'd rather skip the niceties and keep wandering.

Tony waves the boy away, and we take the divergent path into the center of the village. When we reach a little cluster of hostels and outdoor kiosks, we stop to gaze out over the beautiful terraces running up the green mountains. Village life is thriving. The air smells good, earthy and clean, cool and pure, unlike the thick, putrid film that covers the capitol city, Manila. For the first time on this trip I'm glad I came. Maybe Suzanne was right: we all just needed to get outside. We step up to one of the kiosks to buy sodas, and since we are kind enough to carry money in over the mountain, the clerk is kind enough to take it. We sit down at a picnic table to enjoy this little respite.

When Tony wanders off again to gaze dreamily across the view, Suzanne starts in. "Well, what about tonight? What if I want sex? I won't sleep in the same room with him again."

Most of the time I would heel to the suggestion of wild delights with my wife while out adventuring, but she's angry and sour and I can't stomach her. "I don't know," I say. "Can we just be on the trip and put the relationship stuff aside?"

"No," she says, "we can't. I won't sleep in the same room with him again, not while the two of you lust after each other and I'm in the way."

"What?"

"You know what I mean."

"I'm not even going to address this," I say.

I consider that Suzanne is suspicious of me, but I've not yet grown suspicious of her. Truth is, she has already slept with Tony. Perhaps I should be suspicious. Or perhaps I can't find it in me to care. I'm not sure. It seems to me that she's charging me with her impulses. Isn't this projection?

"Doesn't matter. He wants you," she says.

"So what. We're friends only. He knows that."

"I don't care. I won't sleep in there again."

"Have you lost your mind? Why not?"

"Because. I don't have time for it. We've been married two years, and I want a baby."

And there it is. That's the issue, at least a big piece of it: she doesn't really desire me, so it seems, but my seed. She wants my DNA. Here. Now. Wasn't the marriage supposed to be about wanting each other, not a third person who hadn't been created? Or did I have it all wrong? We have been at this stalemate for our entire marriage, so why did she bring this up again here in the Philippines? I consider that maybe she has whipped up a little fantasy about a romantic conception: it all happened while mommy and daddy were young, passionately in love and traveling in exotic lands, she might muse. I felt used.

"I don't want to talk about it," I say.

"You never want to talk about it."

"Not here," I say. "I don't want to talk about it here. I just want to enjoy the trip."

"Here. There. Anywhere. That's the problem. I just want you to promise me you'll have a baby with me. Not right now, but sometime in the future. Next year, maybe. The year after. Even if you don't mean it. I don't care. I just want you to promise me."

"That's crazy," I say. "Promise but not mean it?"

"Why not?" she says. "Just promise me."

She wants me to relieve her anxiety, to promise so she'll be happy and free. The problem is that later, when I betray that promise, she'll blame me for her misery. It won't be her fault that she never had a baby. All along I've doubted that she really wants a baby. I think rather that she wants everything. Or nothing. Or that she has no idea what she wants. Maybe I don't know what I want either. I know one thing: right now I don't want her.

"I already told you I can't promise it. I don't know if I want children. Maybe I don't."

"You will. I know you will. One day you will," she says. "Just promise. That's all I want."

The Ifugao people were fierce headhunters at one time, and I'm wondering if they might not do me a favor. But instead, Tony does me a favor by walking up and interrupting.

"Hey," he says, "what are we planning for tonight? For Y-special-K, I mean."

I frown at him, and he understands why. "I don't know. Any ideas?" I ask, trying to sound cheerful.

"Yeah," he says. "Let's go over to the Banaue Hotel. That big one out there on the edge of town. See what's going on there."

"All right," I say. "Let's do it. Should we start back then?"

"I think we should," Tony says.

Suzanne gets up and heads down the trail.

We ascend through the thick, wispy pines, Suzanne leading as if we don't exist. We pass a little hut where an old man is selling souvenirs to tourists. He offers us a look at his beautiful array of carved wood icons of Bulbul, the Ifugao god that protects the rice harvest. The figure squats on the ground with elbows on knees, chin in hands. He looks calm, almost asleep, and at the same time vigilant. I buy one of them and put it into Tony's backpack. We overtake the Israeli couple and talk briefly with them. They'll be at the Banaue Hotel this evening, too.

It's a long unhappy ride back to town in a jeepney. Suzanne stares out along the edge of the road where we pass hut after hut decorated with roaming chickens and happy children.

III

It is the eve of the new millennium. The Banaue Hotel is not the happeningest place in town. A few dozen foreigners are gathered in the dining room for dinner. Others are in the lobby watching a troupe of Ifugao dancers prostitute themselves for dollars. Still farther off, unmemorable music plays from speakers somewhere in the ceiling. A few people dance.

The walk through town to the hotel was more exciting: people roaming the streets, people igniting fireworks, people belligerent and drunk. We passed a weird little man on a corner playing guitar and singing "Ring of Fire" by Johnny Cash, while a few of his mates danced around him like madmen. No one in Banaue seems worried that their laptops may crash. Or airplanes, for that matter. The only real New Year's danger in the Philippines, Tony reported earlier, is falling bullets (mostly in Manila) from the thousands of people shooting guns into the air.

Suzanne and I have hardly said ten words since Batad, but now she takes my hand and leads me to the dance floor. "Let's dance and forget it," she says.

I go, unwilling at first, suspicious. This is just another ploy to get me into bed, I think. She'll get me drunk and I'll wake up with a houseful of children. Then I check myself: isn't she supposed to want to get me into bed? And I her? We are married, after all. We dance close to a slow song, and I'm reminded of our wedding night. We danced then, too, on and on, until, disturbed by the live band, the uninvited neighbors called the cops.

Suzanne says, "I'm sorry about this afternoon."

"Yeah," I say.

"I mean, I don't want you to feel pressured about having a baby," she says. "Really, I don't."

"OK," I say. "I believe you."

"I mean, I love you," she says. "And it's you I want. A baby would be something beautiful we create together. You know?"

"OK," I say.

"Are you listening to me?"

"Yes," I say, but I'm looking over at the Israeli couple dancing next to us. He is balding and fit, has a hard, handsome jaw. She is smallish with a soft, lacy mouth and beautifully muscled arms. She has Uma Thurman's eyes and hair. All I know of them from our previous meetings is that he is an airline pilot, she a lawyer. They have no children. For a moment I wonder what it would be like to be mixed up in their triangle instead of the one I'm in. But then, I don't want to be in a triangle at all. I don't want to be in anything. Suzanne is still talking, but I can't hear her.

The music ends and I say, "Let's go watch those Ifugao dancers over there."

We go, and Tony comes with us. The dancers are graceful and smiley, dressed in flowing reds and blacks, feathers and bones. I strike up a conversation with Tony.

We're talking about our mutual wanderlust, that impulse that drives us both to believe that everything will be all right if only we were somewhere else, or with someone else. We talk about the pleasures and pain of "The Road," its solitary exultation, its debilitating loneliness. But I'm married now, I say to Tony. Shouldn't I give all that up? He considers, but offers nothing. I don't know if I can, I tell him. Maybe it's my nature to wander. Or maybe wandering is an affliction I have, and there is no cure.

"If it is, c'est la fucking vie," he says.

Now it's his turn, and Tony waxes philosophic about his most recent love affair with a young American man who was also working in the Philippines. He left Tony to wander India like the sages of old. When Tony offered a parting gift, his lover tossed it into the South China Sea. I will keep nothing, the lover said. Own nothing. Tony is deeply wounded by this. He complains. He rails. He desires his lover's return.

I realize this is the conversation I've wanted to have with Tony. This is why I've come. I don't want to pluck out the heart of my own mystery. Not really. I don't want to fix anything, because nothing seems broken. It's just that I can talk plainly with Tony about parts of my nature that I can't explain to Suzanne. The parts I can't seem to get rid of.

Tony looks at his watch. "It's close now. About half an hour—"

"—until the end of the world," I say.

I look around for Suzanne. She's gone.

Tony shrugs. "You'd better go look for her."

I look all around the lobby. I look in the dining room. I look on the dance floor. I wait by the women's restroom for ten minutes. Suzanne is nowhere to be found.

I go outside. I head into town, hoping Suzanne went this way, too. Maybe she's headed back to the room. I walk a half mile or so and find her sitting in the doorway of some darkened building. Her head is in her hands and she's sobbing. I sit down next to her.

"It's almost midnight," I say.

She cries.

"I mean, don't you want to come back for the New Year?"

She looks up at me and cries.

"I'm sorry," I say. "I don't know what else to say. I'm just sorry."

"I should never have come," she says.

"Yeah, maybe," I say. "I thought maybe we could both have what we wanted on this trip. Apparently not."

"No," she says, "I can't have what I want. Anyway, not with you."

For a moment I don't want that to be true. But it is true, and it's a relief to hear it. "Maybe so," I say.

"It's so," she says. "It's been so since we met. It's just that I've not been able to admit it until now."

She's right, of course, and we're doomed. Sitting here on the dark street in Banaue, I'm pretty sure our marriage won't last much longer. "Let's go back for the New Year," I say.

She nods. "All right. I'm ready to go," she says.

We rejoin Tony. Suzanne is better now, and she talks with Tony like she's forgiven him for whatever it was he didn't do. She can be gracious that way, but only part of this graciousness is honest.

The clock ticks down. The Israeli couple joins us, wishes us all a happy New Year. Everyone in the hotel watches the big clock on the wall. The big hand is climbing, climbing, climbing to the top, and then it strikes. The clock dongs, dongs, dongs, twelve times, and the silence between the dongs is deafening as we wait for whatever will happen. An explosion, or the Second Coming, something—but nothing comes. The whole world slides into the next century as everyone in the hotel cheers, and kisses and hugs everyone else, and laughter and clapping travel around the room. Suzanne hugs me in forgiveness. She hugs Tony, too. I hug Tony, and then we all three hug the Israelis, plus a few drunk people who get in our way.

The three of us linger in our little happiness, and then we walk back to the Sanafe Lodge in silence.

Outside, people are everywhere on the roads and in the alleyways, drinking and shouting, lighting firecrackers that flare and burst all around us. Anticipating the long, uncomfortable night in the room, I don't want to stop walking. I want to walk all night, pass through the town and walk until I reach the edge of it, and then step out onto the road, the long rough road to Batad, walk hard and sure, outdistance Suzanne and Tony, and turn up into the wild jungle-mountains of Luzon alone where the villagers do not know me, where, like all the eons before, once again the world has failed to end.

Instructions at the Headwaters

The great Sacramento River wells up from the Earth in a municipal park in Mount Shasta City, California, beneath a choir of Douglas fir and incense cedar. Beyond the springs the river gathers water from the inland slopes of the Klamath Mountains, the Cascade Range, the Coast Range, and the western slope of the Northern Sierra Nevada. The river flows south and west for almost four hundred miles to the Pacific Ocean at San Francisco Bay. Every year (on average) 17.8 million acre-feet of water passes through the city of Sacramento, and 21.6 million acre-feet of water flows into the ocean. This area near the mouth of the river is known locally as "the Delta," and it is a broad tangle of channels and islands and waters.

You may want to walk up behind the place where the Sacramento River emerges from the Earth, just to prove to yourself that the river emerges from the Earth. Go around the waters there, up the steep path (it isn't far) and at the top you'll find a wider pathway leading off in two directions. And nothing more than the dry ground that is the pathway leading off in two directions.

Go a little hungry. If you are satisfied you will be too busy inside and have trouble hearing what the spring might say. Maybe it will say nothing. But this might be what you need to hear most. So go a little hungry. And go in the morning.

To get to the springs, travel to Mount Shasta City and ask around. Almost anyone should know. But be careful to stay on your path. I went to a local climbing shop. When I entered the store, I browsed through the shorts and hiking boots and maps and guidebooks. I also listened in on a story: one of the clerks was walking around in there with his left leg torn from ankle to knee. It was a roughened, meaty mess. He was boasting about his mountain bike crash. He was riding a full-suspension bike for the first time. "Confidence was high!" he quipped, "but skill was low." And he laughed very loud to attract attention, as if that kind of intelligence was something others should acquire. Then I remembered why I was there, and I asked the woman behind the register. She said, "Go north to the edge of town. You will find the springs at the edge of town."

When I arrived I did not see the springs right away. I avoided looking at it. I wanted to save that for later. First I walked behind the springs, just as I have said, to make sure it wasn't some trick. Better to answer that question than leave it rolling around in your mind. If you don't, it might crowd your mind and you won't have a mind for listening.

At the entrance to the springs are two signs. One reads: "No swimming, wading, or bathing in the headwaters. Thank you." The other is a plaque on a drinking fountain that reads: "In honor of Ruby Sullaway Scharff born near here—1885."

Beyond these two signs, the first thing you will notice is the stone retaining wall. The wall holds the river back a little from where it flows out, as if to pool the Earth's heart before it slips away. Where the water is ready to slip away, it flows neatly over and around the wall. I watched a young boy walk across the wall without shoes. Just before that, the boy walked across the top of a picnic table.

I went around to the opposite side of the springs and sat on a large stone near the place where the river emerges from the Earth. An older man approached on foot. I could see him through the trees. He wore his hair long and gray, a beard, and flip-flops on his feet. He removed one flip-flop and looked around. He bent one knee and dragged the naked foot through the cool waters. He put his flip-flop back on and walked away.

A Union Pacific train passed behind the springs. I didn't know the tracks were there! The engine sound was deep like a deep drum, drumming, and I could feel it vibrating in my chest.

Another man approached the springs. He rode in on an old ten-speed bike. He wore regular summer clothes, biking gloves, and a helmet. He leaned his bike against the picnic table and sat down beside the pooling waters. He didn't touch the waters the whole time he was there.

I counted the places against the Earth where the waters flow out. You should try this, too. One. Two. Three. Four. . . . When I got to eight, I noticed the more places I counted, the more places I noticed, smaller and smaller places where the waters flow out. I discovered that what is most true is that the waters do not flow from a certain number of places, but from every place at once. Later, I found these in Dogen:

> Accordingly, even where there is not a river or an ocean, there is water. It is just that when water falls down to the ground, it manifests the characteristics of rivers and oceans.

> However, when most human beings see water they only see that it flows unceasingly. This is a limited human view: there are actually many kinds of flowing.

Two vehicles arrived at the headwaters carrying three people: two women and one boy. The two women looked very similar. They both wore loose fitting cotton pants that moved like flags in the breeze, short summer tops exposing their bellies, and wide-brimmed straw hats. The boy went to the waters and got in. The women unloaded plastic containers of every kind, a vast collection: one six-gallon water can, two five-gallon collapsible water cans, a half dozen Nalgene bottles, and another half dozen, or so, variously sized and shaped plastic bottles. They went to work filling them up. One of the women drank from one of the bottles she filled, and then she filled it again.

I heard around town that some local people come here for water every day, and that they will drink only from the springs. This seems right to me, for we are creatures drawn to the source. Big Spring is cousin to Big Bang, as the waters flow up from the clay that made us.

When all the containers were filled, the women loaded them into their vehicles with the boy, who was drying now in the mountain sun, and they drove away.

Near the edges of the pooling waters are tiny islands of soil. Wild watercress grows here. And a little farther up the bank, horsetail fern. And willow, long fingers of willow, beneath the over-arching branches of Douglas fir and incense cedar.

From the rock where I was sitting I stepped down into the waters. The trees and willow and fern and green came up around me like the dome of a great cathedral. The waters were cold and sharp, coming up over my feet in my sandals, pooling there and going in between my toes. Let's not get overly holy, but here is something again from Dogen:

> On the other hand, from ancient times wise people and sages have often lived near water. When they live near water they catch fish, catch human beings, and catch the way. For long these have been genuine activities in water. Furthermore there is catching the self, catching catching, being caught by catching, and being caught by the way.

I crouched and drank from the headwaters like a cat.

The Best Thing about Marriage Is Divorce

The power of love, as Jung rightly surmised, resides in the abnega-
tion of the power principle. Though we may will that a relationship
continue indefinitely, we may discover, contrary to our wishes, that
we must sacrifice a union . . . or lose our capacity to love.

GREG MOGENSON

Well, some time after that we came to divorce. We had been at the
edge of it several times, Suzanne and I, but this time we put it
on for real, like a warm coat on a cold day. And we tried to undo it later,
promise each other everything, for that is what crazed people do, like
high altitude climbers gone out of their heads with hypothermia and
hypoxia—they strip off their clothes and are found dead-frozen on the
mountainside in the nude. We would go beyond that, though, beyond the
place of fearing the road ahead, out so far that we couldn't make it back.
Would that not be the easiest kind of dying? The one where you faced off
with the empty desert too far to walk across, and you just start walking,
no food or water or supplies of any kind. Or try the great Pacific. Get in.
Swim out to the limit of your endurance, and then that's it. You have
no choice but to go through with it—you can't make it back. Nothing
you do now will allow you to fall victim to your own fear and pull out.

For that is what it is, that is what keeps people together who desire or need to be apart: fear. That one word, which is not a word only, but the most terrible kind of darkness. You fear loneliness, maybe most of all. You fear heartache. You fear the loss of familiar patterns. The realization that you are no longer young strikes you very hard now, and you come to an undeniable truth: this life is for real. By "real" I mean that divorce can help you understand—in a way not possible before—that you are going to die, one day. A broken heart can do that for you. And then something more comes after this. After you have moved through fear, survived it, and have been released on the other side, why, then, you also realize that the best thing about your marriage was divorce.

Cheyenne, Wyoming, USA
December 2003

"So, do you want to be the plaintiff or the defendant?" I asked.

"The defendant," Suzanne said. "You're divorcing me."

"No I'm not. You tried to divorce me more times that I tried to divorce you," I said. "At least a dozen. I'm just admitting that I can't be or do whatever it is you want."

"But that was in anger," she said. "I was just angry all those times. I didn't mean it. I didn't really want to divorce you."

"Oh," I said. "Well, I thought you meant it. That's why you locked yourself in the bathroom for four hours and wouldn't come out."

"I was angry," she said again. "That's all. Besides, I had to stay in there. You wouldn't leave me alone. I needed to be alone."

"I know. I should have left you alone. And you also meant it. If you'll remember, it was me who brought us back all those times. It was me who kept us together through all that. You wanted out. Every time."

"You did bring us back, but don't think that you meant it," she said.

"What? Are you crazy?"

"You didn't mean it. You wanted out just as much as I did," she said. "You just couldn't bring yourself to admit it."

"Well, yeah. When you were acting crazy I was desperate to get out."

"No, you were just desperate to get out. Why can't you admit that?"

"ok, you're right. I admit it. What does it matter now anyway. I wanted out too," I said.

"Then why didn't you let it happen? I gave you all those chances. I tried to divorce you, and you wouldn't let me."

"Wouldn't let you? How can you say that? You could have done it if you'd wanted. Why didn't you? I wish you had."

"Don't say that," she said.

"Why not? We're getting a divorce anyway. What does it matter? I just wish you had been stronger and gone through with it."

"Now *you're* crazy," she said. "If you wanted a divorce, all you had to do was ask for it."

"Oh yeah. Right," I said. "You're right. I guess neither of us wanted to be the one who did it."

"I don't want to fight with you," she said.

"I'm not fighting. We're talking, aren't we?"

"We're fighting."

"No we're not. At least I'm not. See, this was always a problem too. We could never talk without you accusing me of fighting."

"I don't want to fight with you," she said.

"OK. And I don't want to fight with you either," I said. "Let's just do this."

"All right," she said. "OK. So, I still want to be the defendant."

"OK," I said. "I'll be the plaintiff. It's easier that way, I guess, since I'll be handling all the paperwork."

"You got it then?"

"Yeah. It was so easy, and it only cost me ten bucks. The instructions are all here. We're lucky we're doing this now instead of last year. Divorcing in California would have been a nightmare."

"Yeah," she agreed. "We're lucky."

Air Canada Flight 51, over Kabul, Afghanistan
November 2003

Before that, I went to India to visit a new women's college in a minor village near the place the sacred Ganges flows out from the foothills of the Himalayas. I never imagined that coming to Wyoming would take me to India, but it did. The story is that a man named Vinod Gupta, who grew up in that village, found his way to the University of Nebraska. From there he started a company that made him very wealthy, and he decided to use some of his good fortune to improve the lives of his people back home. This was cutting-edge thinking (much like the company Gupta founded), for women had few opportunities for higher education in India. In fact, practically none. He assembled an august team (that included a community college president in Nebraska) to build a vocational college for women, especially women from rural areas. Shrimati Ram Rati Gupta Women's Polytechnic, named after Gupta's late mother, opened in 2000. Gupta has since built other institutions in Rampur: the Bill Clinton Science and Technology Center, to honor his close friend, the former president; and the Hillary Rodham Clinton Mass Communication Center. The community college president from Nebraska later became executive director of the Wyoming Community College Commission. As an English instructor at a Wyoming community college, I was selected to be one of three delegates to travel to the Polytechnic to work on curriculum and programs.

I flew to Delhi a few days after I told Suzanne, at last, that I wanted a divorce. It wasn't a happy scene, and terribly inconvenient. She had a couple old friends visiting, and I was about to leave the country. I would have rather waited until I returned. But I had made the decision, and there wasn't any hiding it from her. She was far too intuitive for her own good. She asked, and I told her, and then came the wailing and shouting and the "I can't go on without you," etc. It surprised me. She had divorced me so many times already, I expected relief in her voice, not resistance. I was quite certain this was the right path, and I held steady for most of the night. But Suzanne was persuasive, and so we agreed to talk again when I returned. Let's just suspend everything right here with this conversation, we said. Let's not take any action quite yet.

I carried a terrible guilt with me to India—wasn't it callous and selfish to be making this trip while my marriage teetered on the edge? And yet, going or not, I admitted, my marriage still teetered on the edge. There was a lot of teetering. In other news, perhaps the time away would allow some clarity, a space apart to really affirm that we were doing the right thing. The same can be achieved with bi-weekly visits to a therapist: you dork out five thousand dollars to find out what you already know. I'll take the journey to India any day. But at Suzanne's insistence, I did the other, too.

From Toronto it was nearly fifteen hours to Delhi, the longest by an hour that I had ever been on an airplane. The pilot announced that we would fly over Kabul but that we would be way too high for most surface-to-air missiles. Next to me were my two companions, Jan and Ann, both from Eastern Wyoming Community College. Ann was the college vice president and dean of instruction, and Jan directed the fitness center and taught P.E. They were both small-town girls with big-town vision. Ann was soft-spoken, jowly, and a voracious reader. Jan had never been out of North America. She would shoot over nine hundred photographs with her fancy digital camera. They both wore their hair exceedingly short, while I wore mine long. This would become a topic of some inquiry at the Polytechnic. Was this the way things worked in America, some of the students asked. Did women have short hair and men long hair? I loved the idea of busting the standard. Jan carried a big bag filled with snacks from home, which she dug into and offered around liberally. I munched on peanuts and chocolate while reading *The Songlines*, page after page, stalling out in the section called "From the Notebooks," those beautiful passages from various sources about travel, wanderlust, nomads, walking, Cain and Abel. I sang to myself a little freedom song tinged with guilt:

Oh I'm a little wandering guy . . .
up here in the beautiful sky . . .
I'll never go home again.
Goodbye, Suzanne. Goodbye.

Well, actually, I didn't sing that song, but the feeling that comes in those words (two parts bitterness, one part liberty), the idea of myself as a free, indestructibly happy wanderer, resonated inside me and helped to cheer me up.

Somewhere into hour eleven my two companions and I each had our *Lonely Planet* guides open: a row of little blue covers with green sashes. I was reading up on Roop Kanwar, the eighteen-year-old girl who committed sati in Rajasthan on September 4, 1987; she burned to death on her dead husband's funeral pyre. The couple had been married for less than a year. In a traditional Indian marriage the husband is lord, or pati, and a good wife practices pativrata, total devotion to the husband. She worships him by eating his leftovers. If he dies, what is she to do? Sati is an extension of this devotion. The act of self-immolation glorifies the husband and elevates the selfless widow to a goddess. A shrine is built on the location of her sacrifice, and she is worshipped forever after. The word "sati" means "a chaste woman." The practice, most common among the Rajput people of Rajasthan, was banned by the British in 1829, but it has continued quietly, though perhaps less frequently, ever since. This particular case sparked a national controversy. Many people spoke out against it. A barbaric act, they said, that violates women's rights worldwide. Traditionalists (many of them women) spoke out in support of the practice. They founded the Committee for the Defense of the Religion of Sati. Within one week of Roop Kanwar's death, my *Lonely Planet* reports, the site was attracting worshippers by the tens of thousands. Divorce is almost unheard of in India, even in cases of extreme domestic violence, because divorced women, along with widows, are shunned and prevented from remarrying. Like the Japanese practice of seppuku, sati allows a widow to die with honor and escape a deplorable solitary existence. An added value is that the woman who commits sati guarantees her husband and seven generations of her family a passport to heaven.

What struck me most deeply in reading this story was not the ethical position I immediately formed against the practice—Roop Kanwar's death was brutal, unconscionable, and preventable—but how dramatically marriage has changed in recent times. Until the eighteenth century, in most places on the globe marriage was primarily a political and economic alliance (as it likely was in Roop Kanwar's case), and partners were chosen by families rather than the individuals "getting married." Divorce was rare because partners relied on each other for practical reasons, for survival rather than for love. This is still largely the case in India and other places. Of course, yes, the power in the family was/is centered in the husband, and wives had/have little recourse or choice. On the extreme edge, this condition allows but does not encourage spousal abuse, and even murder. This can't be good. I'm against such stories, too. But, to counterbalance these ills, consider how wide the pendulum has swung. We Americans are especially hard-lined in our belief that we're a liberated nation when it comes to love and marriage. With Platonic fealty our mission is to seek and find that one individual God made only for us. He or she is out there somewhere, we believe, and when the moment is right (perhaps when God finds us ready or worthy—is this *the one?*), a chance meeting will result in a tender courtship, love, marriage, children, and "joy and union without end," as Milton put it. This pious attitude has Americans looking to their marriage partners to fulfill *all* needs and desires: emotional, spiritual, sexual, intellectual, and financial. Who can live up to that? Furthermore, researchers say, such reliance on our spouses often results in a separation from our communities. Our sphere of friendships atrophies, and soon not only do we look to our spouse for everything, but our spouse is the only one left to look to. No wonder over half of all marriages in the United States end in divorce and, paradoxically, the rate is even higher in the Bible Belt.

Cheyenne, Wyoming, USA
December 2003

"I want to keep the photograph you gave me for Christmas," Suzanne said.

"Of course," I said. "Of course. It's yours. It was a gift."

It really was a beautiful photograph. Matted and framed, measuring about twenty-four by forty inches, it features a White River Apache girl in ceremonial dress undergoing the final moments of her four-day rite-of-passage ceremony, the ceremony in which an Apache girl becomes a woman. In the photograph she is seated with her right arm resting on her thigh, her hand open, palm up. Her eyes are closed though she is looking upward, the sun's light raining down on her. Her hair and face, shoulders and dress are painted with earth paint, a mixture of clay and water. The earth paint symbolizes her acceptance of the power of the Earth, the power of Changing Woman, one of the holy people and the first Apache. Of this moment and this ceremony, the photographer, Stephen Trimble, has written, "I have never seen anything more moving."

I had to admit that I wanted to keep the photograph for myself. I had taken such pains to buy it at silent auction, and then to have it matted and framed. I had felt so good about giving it to Suzanne, about how the object expressed the best part of her, expressed who she was and what she valued most in this world. It honored her beyond me, beyond our marriage. It was a photograph of the way Suzanne was rooted in place and community, the way she strived always for self-actualization, especially spiritually and emotionally, and the most intimate expression of this identity was part of the reason we were divorcing—Suzanne wanted a baby and I did not. But I found the expression of this beautiful, how the object and the woman were one thing. I wanted to keep the idea of that beauty. In that instant I wondered why I wasn't entitled to the photograph. Besides, it seemed to belong there on the wall of this little log house we'd bought together west of Cheyenne less than a year before. The next thought in my mind was that yes, of course the photograph was Suzanne's. There was no question that it was hers. Besides, I reminded myself, she would get the artwork but I would be taking the wall it was hanging on; I would be taking the cabin.

"What else?" I asked. "What else is important to you?"

"Let's talk about the kitchen," Suzanne said. "Those pots and pans. Your parents really gave them as a gift to me."

"Yes," I said. "That's right."

I marked that down on paper. We were making a record of what we agreed on. I would then write a formal letter detailing our agreement, and we'd both sign it and keep a copy. We didn't want to end up fighting later over the few material goods we had.

"I'd like to keep the down comforter and pillows my mom gave us," I said. "I don't know why."

"OK," she said. "Thank you for telling me that that means something to you. Can we do the whole kitchen first? Maybe we should proceed room by room so we don't get mixed up."

"That's sensible," I said.

We were being very careful to be generous, to be attentive to each other's feelings, desires, fears, something we mostly failed at during our marriage.

"So I want the mixer. It's my color, you know. And it was also really a gift to me."

"Yes. What else?"

"The knives."

"Okay," I said, saying good-bye to those beautiful German kitchen knives. "Anything else in the kitchen?"

"The blender matches the mixer, you know. And I want the coffee maker too."

After the kitchen, we made a walk through the rest of the house, each of us pointing out items we wanted, negotiating their value against something the other would get. We wanted to make it even, that most of all, so neither of us would come to contesting the divorce. Why give what little money and assets we did have to a couple lawyers and come out of a fight with nothing, when we could just split it down the middle? We would handle our taxes the same way. If we filed as a married couple we could split the substantial return. If we filed separately while still married, we'd each have to pay. It was in both our interests to cooperate, to compromise. But there was something more, and Suzanne brought us back to this again and again. Compromise, she insisted, was also about our emotional health. If we did this right, if we cared for each other during the divorce, we could each move on with our lives more quickly, more freely. We could let the other go, and so be released. That was far more valuable than a few thousand dollars worth of appliances.

We would each keep our own pickups, both paid for. We would each keep our individual debts (student loans and the like), and our savings (retirement packages and savings accounts). Because I was taking over the mortgage on the house, I took the larger items that a house required: the washer and dryer, the refrigerator, the bed, the table and chairs. Over the past year Suzanne had made a home for herself in Boulder where she was finishing her psychology masters program at Naropa University. She wanted those items that were more mobile, easier to move. She took her four-thousand-dollar mountain bike, of course, both Yakima bike racks, the popup camper on her truck, and her light touring canoe.

"I want the Rampage, too," she said.

"What do you mean?" I asked. "My white water boat?" Or at least, until that moment, it was my white water boat.

"Yes," she said. "I want it."

We bought it together, I was sure she would remind me, but it was a boat I had wanted for a long time, a boat I thought Suzanne had no interest in. Why did she want to keep it? She couldn't even paddle it effectively, and every time she'd been in it, she cussed it all the way down the river. I imagined the boat would mostly sit next to a house somewhere in Boulder and rot in the sun. I wanted to fight with her on this point.

"I thought it was mine." I said.

"It's not yours," she said. "It's *ours*. And I want it."

"Why? I thought you didn't like it."

"I never said that."

"Okay, but you never seemed to like paddling it."

"Yeah, but now I want it," she said.

"I want it too," I said.

"Look, you get the entire house. I want the boat."

"It's a debt. I get the mortgage, not the house."

"You know what I mean. You could sell this place and make way more than that boat is worth. Plus, you love this cabin. And you've wanted to live here alone since we bought it."

"Since I bought it, you mean."

"We bought it *to-ge-ther*," she said, using all three syllables, for she was a wordsmith too.

"It was my money," I said. "We agreed to split that money from the California house, and you spent your half on school. I invested mine in this cabin."

"Oh, now that's why were divorcing, right there."

"I thought it was over babies?"

"That, too," she said. "I'm taking the boat. Get over it."

"Plus, since I'm paying you half the equity, that means you're taking three quarters of the California money, and leaving me one quarter."

"I'd rather not bring up the past," she said. "Can't we just deal with our situation now?"

"I see, when the past is against you, let's not bring it up."

"Look, I could get a lot more if I wanted, and I should, according to some people I've talked to. But I'm not asking for your retirement accounts. Or anything else. Get over it. I'm taking the boat."

I hated being threatened, but she was right. I had to get over it. I wanted the house, and I didn't want to do battle. But somewhere in my mind, I decided later, that boat represented my dog. Maybe because Osa often rode along in front with me as we negotiated little drops and rapids. It was Osa's boat as much as mine. Maybe because I believed Suzanne had taken Osa from me, and that now in my time of need, when the house was about to empty out and I'd be left alone, I didn't even have my dog for company. Now she wanted my boat too? I guess I was still very angry about what happened.

I was in Vermont a winter ago, and both dogs were in Boulder with

Suzanne. I say both dogs, as we had taken on litter mates from our neighbors in California. Lily had bonded with Suzanne, and Osa with me. We had separate vehicles, separate money and bank accounts, separate dreams, separate dogs. They were blue-heeler and McNab crosses, highly intelligent, beautiful, fine endurance. Down in Boulder, in a moment of strange circumstance, Osa went out the front door of Suzanne's rental house and never came back. Later a city cop found her wrecked body out on Highway 36. I'm certain she was headed home to Wyoming. Losing a dog is maybe like losing a hand or an eye—you're just not sure if all your parts work the right way anymore. It's the one thing about my relationship with Suzanne I don't know how to forgive.

I still didn't want to fight, though, and I drummed up the numerous reasons the boat wasn't worth my time: the outfitting was no good, never had been; those vinyl decks that came a quarter of the way to the cockpit, I didn't like; and the boat had a stupid name, the "Rampage." Too shredder. Too adrenaline cowboy. She could have the "Ram-page." It would fit her uppity Boulder life anyway. Good-bye little boat.

"It's yours," I said. "What's next?"

"That's it, I think," Suzanne said.

"Well, I'll type this up and send you a copy. So, can we look over these papers then before you drive back to Boulder?"

"OK," she said. "But let's hurry. It's late."

"You have to sign this one and acknowledge that I served you."

"You never served me, that's for sure," she said.

I laughed. I couldn't remember her ever trying to be funny. In our marriage she was always so serious, so self-help, so bent on utopia. She was always talking about being "in relationship," a phrase I despised but then later began using myself. She was always instructing me on what was and what was not "a feeling." I'd say something like, "I feel like you're never happy with what I do for you." And then she'd yell back at me, "That's not a feeling!" Anyway, I guess we really did stifle each other.

"No, I mean—"

"I know," she said, smiling. I thought I could see my little blue boat gleaming in her eyes. "It has to be notarized, right?"

"Yeah."

"Probably too late for tonight, don't you think?"

"I know a place," I said. "It closes at nine. Why don't you follow me into town, and then you can go on to Boulder from there."

"OK," she said. "Let's go."

Haridwar, Uttaranchal, India
November 2003

Barefooted, I stood on the ghat in the sacred waters of the Ganges. The river, revered as a goddess, rose up around my ankles to wash away all my sins, and everywhere I looked there were people, people by the thousands thronging the Har-ki-Pairi, or the Footstep of God, the place the river flows out from the Himalayas. Here Vishnu, the preserver, the sustainer of all that is good in the universe, left his footprint, it is said, and the river flows from his feet. From his feet to mine. The priest who attended me held a little green boat made out of woven leaves and filled with pretty flowers—the lotus, I wondered, as Vishnu always appears with the lotus blossom, the navel of the universe. It is fragile and also enduring; it can grow, even flourish in the foulest of waters. The priest spoke out a blessing in a language I did not know, and then asked me to repeat the blessing after him. He spoke again, pausing to listen to me stumble through the words. That done, he lit the candle seated on the nest of flowers.

"Now is your turn to ask a prayer," he said. "In your own language. Whatever you want."

"I wish . . . I want," I said in a whisper, for I hadn't thought to prepare anything, "a quiet life in the mountains." Of course, I thought of Suzanne, but I left her out.

The priest set the leafy boat into the river washing over my feet, released it, and away it went downstream, swirling and mingling with the many lights of other boats, other people's dreams. Just a few feet away I could see Pooja, one of the teachers from the Polytechnic, accompanying the three of us on this day-trip to Haridwar and Rishikesh (the self-proclaimed yoga capital of the world). We had waited all day for this, the Ganga Aarti, the river blessing ceremony. The priest at Pooja's side bent and released her little boat of dreams, and away it went with mine.

A man stepped forward on a platform behind me—I just caught his movement in my eye—and something flew from his hand. It splashed down in the sacred river. Another offering of some sort, I wondered, another prayer? No. A gallon-sized paint can. It swirled away in the current, tipped and filled, and sank to the bottom. You see, there was a crew of men working on a building behind us. What else were they to do with the garbage?

"Now, then," the priest said, "how much you wish to give?"

"Give?" I said.

"Yes, for your wishes? Did you wish it for your family? How many of them are there?"

"Give what to who?" I said.

"What will you give for the blessing for all your family? You give me what you think is enough for them."

"Oh, you want money," I said. Very little could get by me.

"Well, donation for your wishes. That's all. I suggest 200. That is good for your whole family."

I had no idea what was fair. At the current rate, 200 rupees was about four dollars. "How about 50," I said.

"For your whole family? Only that? How much you love them?" he said.

"Seventy-five?"

"Two hundred is best," he said. "Very cheap."

I looked around hoping to see what others were paying. I looked for Pooja, but she wasn't there. "I'll give you 100," I said.

"For your whole family? Surely they are worth more."

"One hundred," I said.

"OK," the priest said, smiling. "That is a fine price, yes. That will bless everyone."

I walked back up the steps of the ghat feeling happy and pure, relieved of all my guilt. Jan and Ann were waiting for me with Smeeta and Pagirut, the driver, and now Pooja was there.

"Did you enjoy it?" Smeeta asked.

"Oh yes," I said. "Thank you. Really wonderful."

"What did you pay?" Pooja asked.

"One hundred?" I said. "How much did you pay?"

"Twenty," she said, giggling.

That night at the Hotel Punjab in Saharanpur, a wedding erupted in the ballroom on the floor beneath me. All night it raged, music and loud voices and clanging cymbals. A rich celebration for the ages, while outside in the sultry night the myriad poor and destitute passed by slowly on the road, or lay about in stinking corners near the garbage piles, where stray dogs fought with feral urban pigs over scraps of who knows what from who knows where. At every turn it was poverty next to wealth, sorrow next to the general gaiety of the Indian people. I barely got any sleep. But it had been so every night in the Hotel Punjab, for it was the season of weddings in India, when the stars were aligned just so, so that anyone who had to, might as well.

"Oh, yes, Indian weddings are very loud," said Raj Kamal, the Polytechnic's principal. "Would you like to attend one tonight? One of our teachers is getting married, as it happens."

We did attend, and Raj was right, it was very loud. Unfortunately for the bride, it meant that she would have to abandon her teaching career for a life of household duties. "This Polytechnic is like a family for me," she told me. "I can't live to miss it too much." The two families had agreed on the wedding long ago, and a good wife would obey the wishes of her new husband. Somewhere in the midst of all that I found a moment to write an e-mail message to Suzanne: "I am so far outside this marriage," I wrote, "I don't know how to get back in."

After a couple weeks at the Polytechnic, Ann, Jan, and I condensed our notes and observations about the college's programs and presented them to Raj, then off we went on the train back to Delhi. We spent a day touring the Taj Mahal, an icon of perfect love. Removing our shoes, we walked barefooted across the brilliant white marble terraces and through the shades of the slender upshot minarets. The main Taj is an immense white water drop, as if marble slipped liquid out of heaven. It really is as striking as they say. Built by Emperor Shah Jahan as a final resting place for his beloved second wife, Mumtaz Mahal, one poet captured the Taj with this line: "A tear on the cheek of time." Speaking of icons of love, coincidentally, President Clinton had arrived in Delhi a few days earlier for a conference on AIDS. A group of students and faculty from the Polytechnic, along with Vin Gupta, met him as he arrived at his hotel.

"What did he say when you shook his hand?" I had asked Deepali, an open and radiant woman who taught in the nursery and primary teacher's training program at the Polytechnic.

"Oh, well," she blushed. "I asked him if he wasn't tired from his long travels. And he said me, 'Yes, I was tired. But now I am not, not now, surrounded by all these beautiful Indian girls.'"

I wouldn't know it for another few days, but Suzanne had already moved out of the Wyoming cabin. She was in Boulder for good now, and all we had left were the details of the end. When I came home from those many hours in flight, the house would be dark and it wouldn't get light again for a long time.

That night, after touring the Taj, fifteen thousand couples married in Delhi. What sounded to me like extravagance was merely routine. In India, in these gentle winter months, when the stars foretell good fortune, the city prepares the way.

Cheyenne, Wyoming
December 2003

An hour after we had split up our worldly goods, I led Suzanne into the parking lot of the Sportsman's Outlet on Lincolnway. She pulled in behind me in her truck, parked, got out.

"Here?" she said, turning up her lip. "You want me to get this notarized here?"

"Yeah. This guy's a notary public. He has to be to sell guns. He'll charge you two bucks. It'll just take a minute."

But before I could finish she turned away from me and headed for the door.

I waited outside in the night. It was cold but there was surprisingly little wind. I leaned against my dirty truck, taking on a bit of the engine warmth. Cheyenne, the largest city in Wyoming at fifty-three thousand people, didn't impose much in the way of light pollution, and I could see the stars spread thinly over that immense black space. There was Orion in the dark and lonely emptiness, and that point of light below Orion's belt, the Orion Nebula, where stars were being born. And there, that great band of light which we are part of, the Milky Way, revolving forever around a mathematical equation, a black hole, that is, a singularity through which one might journey to another where and another when. Back on Earth, I imagined Suzanne inside the Sportman's Outlet with the proprietor, his little black mustache twitching, his notary kit on the glass counter over all those shiny hand guns. Maybe a Browning Hi-Power 9 mm with Dutch connections would be staring up at Suzanne through the glass, or a Bond Arms Texas Defender .45 Colt, perhaps even a Smith & Wesson Model 21-4 Thunder Ranch .44 Special in a wood presentation box. How much luckier could she get? Out in front of her would be rows of gleaming shotguns and rifles—maybe something high-end, like the Ithaca Classic Doubles Superlative 2 Barrel Set Game Gun, firing both 20 and 16 gauge; or a Winchester Model 12 Feather Weight 12 gauge. Maybe she'd be staring at a Mannlicher Shoenauer .30-06 MC Sporting Rifle with Zeiss scope next to a Poly Tech Chinese AK-47. But what did I know.

It wasn't long before the door of the shop opened and Suzanne came out. Something was different about her now. Something was missing. She was walking funny, sorta shambling too fast across the parking lot without her usual boldness or confidence. She came up to me and we stood facing each other in silence. I thought we were about to look up at the beautiful night sky and acknowledge, like so many heroic movie couples in moments of duress, that there was a great deal of poverty and suffering available in the world, that we were but tiny creatures on a pale blue dot floating in an immense and unknowable universe, and so, though divorce wasn't easy, our problems were really not that big-a-deal. But Suzanne's shoulders slumped forward, her back and arms began to quake, and the tears came loose. Some inhuman sound came out of her, and then her words, which were separated and joined in all the wrong places: "I just got divorced in a gun shop."

I held her then until she recovered herself, and there were tears for me, too. It was strange, this kind of love, where outside the legal document that is marriage we came to care deeply for each other without expectation. She no longer wanted anything from me and in turn I no longer wanted anything from her. Our desires and dreams did not hinge on the other's behest. We were completely free, and we freely held each other in the dark, just two weak human beings acknowledging how painful, how joyous it is to get on in this world. And then I felt an odd interjection, a powerful desire to return to that same condition from which I was fleeing—marriage. Standing there in the Wyoming night with Suzanne in my arms, her breath and heart-warmth against me, her hair sweet-smelling and girlish, her hands tenderly grasping at me, I thought at last we'd come to the truth of it and we didn't really have to get divorced after all. How could feelings as powerful as these ever fade?

A rush of lights and engines came by on Lincolnway, and the cold night returned to us with the notarized divorce papers still in Suzanne's hand. She held them out to me. I accepted them. We parted. She got into her truck, I got into mine, and we drove out. I followed her for a little distance until we reached that place where my road continued west and her road turned south. I pulled up beside her at the intersection. We looked at each other through the glass. We waved.

Wild Man at Iouzan

Who takes the Cold Mountain Road
takes a road that never ends
the rivers are long and piled with rocks
the streams are wide and choked with grass
it's not the rain that makes the moss slick
and it's not the wind that makes the pines moan
who can get past the tangles of the world
and sit with me in the clouds
HAN SHAN, translated by Red Pine

I met the Wild Man looking out over the sea from the summit of Iouzan on the Shiretoko Peninsula in Hokkaido, Japan. He stood into the wind, his fly open, his black hair on end, his beard unkempt and peppered with his age. His eyes were wild and cliché, like Coleridge's Mariner or the Sumerian wild man, Enkidu, who roamed with the beasts, his eyes with a far-off nearby look, slightly agitated, possibly mad, evermore happy to be here on top of a great mountain.

"Hello. Hello. Hello!" he sang out to me as I humped the final steps to the summit. "Oh, hello there American guy!" he said. Obviously he'd had some practice with English.

"Hello," I called back to him. "Beautiful day, isn't it?"

"Oh yes. Beautiful! Beautiful!" he agreed. "Yes, very beautiful."

And it was beautiful. The cool dry air deepened my view north into the Sea of Okhotsk and, behind me, the far green mountain country that was Shiretoko. I felt at ease, and happy to be there too.

But that's not how I felt earlier that morning starting out with my two companions. At the trailhead at 7:00 a.m. the temperature had already reached 35 degrees Centigrade (about 95 Fahrenheit) and it was horridly humid. The northernmost of Japan's four major islands, Hokkaido, is the driest and coolest, but this summer many of the refreshing storms had missed the island and spun off into Korea. Five minutes on the trail and I was pouring sweat. Great circles showed under the arms of my drab brown polypro T-shirt, and sweat spread across my chest and back. I hated humidity. Maybe living for almost a decade in desert places had something to do with it.

Watanabe, a barber from Kitami, wrapped his head in a white towel to stop the sweat from running into his eyes and blinding him. Noguchi, my good friend who I had met nine years earlier when I worked as an English teacher in a small town an hour south of Sapporo, rolled his nylon pants up to his knees and put on a cap to keep the intrepid sun from searing his balding pate. I didn't have a towel or a hat. And I wore a pair of heavy cotton Carharts. I carried a pair of shorts in my backpack, but I was too much in denial to put them on. I donned my sunglasses and prayed the climb would help me shake my bad attitude. Thus outfitted, we started up the mountain.

Shiretoko National Park is arguably Japan's wildest landscape. The word "Shiretoko" means "End of the World" in the language of Hokkaido's indigenous Ainu people. The peninsula is graced by a chain of rugged mountains, the highest of which range from 1,254 to 1,660 meters (4,113 to 5,444 feet). That's not high compared to Colorado's "14ers," but these mountains rise straight up out of the sea, as do the trails that lead to their summits. Shiretoko is also famous for its population of brown bears, some six hundred strong. The Ainu people draw much of their cultural and spiritual identity from the bear. Hot springs are another attraction on Shiretoko, especially the famous Kamuiwakka-no-Taki or "waterfall of the gods." Visitors can walk straight up the streambed to successively hotter and hotter pools. It's one of the few hot springs in

Japan where people wear clothing. When I inquired about this point on our visit, Noguchi explained: "It's mixed bathing. Many beautiful womans there. Nobody do it, but naked is maybe no problem. Please try, if you have a confidence."

I didn't.

The trail up the mountain angled across a steep slope through the trees, then broke out onto a blazing hot boulder field. Everywhere sulfurous steam leaked from invisible volcanic vents. It made my eyes water, my stomach queasy. Then we turned up the ridge through a jungle of weird bushy pines that stretched on as far as we could see. I was miserable in that dark tunnel of trees, branches everywhere grazing my sweat-frothed skin.

Watanabe moaned about his cramping legs. Noguchi said we'd be at the top soon. I told him, think again, and pointed to the summit that seemed to rise out of an impossible distance. We'd never make it, I was certain. Why did we want to make it anyway? There was nothing special about Iouzan. We were climbing for climbing's sake, or for exercise, or to stave off boredom, which might be fine in good weather, but for me the novelty of suffering this brutal humidity was wearing out. I couldn't shake my desire to be home in cool, dry Wyoming, drinking cold beer on my porch.

So why had I come? When I left Hokkaido nine years earlier, I vowed to return as often as possible. I had loved my two and a half years here, and so wanted to always be in touch with the landscape, the people, the lifestyle. But as way leads on to way, I couldn't seem to get back. Life was happening to me whether I liked it or not. Upon leaving Hokkaido I accepted another teaching gig that evolved into a teaching career, wrapped up two master's degrees, got married, got divorced, decided once and for all not to have children, gave away a dog I loved, buried another, and lived in ten different houses in five different states, not to mention the bilateral hernia surgery and my ex-wife's insistence that therapy would transform me into the man she had always wanted.

But that's not quite right. We loved each other, admired each other, drew a spiritual strength from each other. We did everything right together, except marriage. We could never find common ground in sharing and managing finances, physical space in the house, our vision of our future, or, especially, children. She wanted children fiercely and passionately. I did not. And so we ended it, still in love.

During those years of marital wrangling, Hokkaido persisted in my mind like a dirty secret. I had been so free of cares in Japan. I had more money than I needed and no bills or debts. I had the kind of fame that comes with being a foreigner in a small curious town. Every day was like a party. Could life get any better?

In the aftermath of my divorce I wondered if a trip back to Hokkaido was what I needed to renew myself, to regain that beautiful freedom. At the very least I'd be able to visit old friends and old haunts, walk up a few mountains, drink beer and sake, feast on meat and rice for days on end. It would be just like old times.

Now here I was in Hokkaido, doing exactly what I had dreamed of and generally hating every minute of it.

At the notch high above tree line the cooler air renewed my hope, but Watanabe gave up. He threw himself down dramatically as if never to rise again. Noguchi and I dropped our packs and continued on, climbing the final steep trail through the rocks and up, up, really climbing now, holding onto the mountain face with our hands, while off to our left a sheer rock face fell a thousand feet back into that dreaded humidity.

"I don't like high place," Noguchi said, his hands visibly shaking.

"It's a little late for that," I said back to him. "Come on. We're really close now."

And we were. A few more steps and we were standing on the summit.

"How'd you know I was American?" I asked the Wild Man. I wore my be-sweated hair pulled back in a ponytail, Italian boots, my brown, sweat-soaked polypro t-shirt, and the shorts, also brown, which I had finally put on half way up. I looked like a plate of unappetizing food, all of it the same color.

"Oh, just guessing," he said, chipping at the mountain with his ice axe. Ice axe? There was no snow anywhere. "Maybe you're American."

"Right," I said.

"Where from?" he asked, walking right up to me. I stood at least eight inches taller than he did. I could see the top of his wild, black head, but somehow he seemed very large, or he made me feel very small.

"Wyoming," I mustered.

"Wy-oming," he said in his deep, resonant voice. "Oh, Grand-O-

Tetons!" He cupped his chest with his hands. "I speak French. Grand-O-Tetons. Like a woman, you know?"

"Yes, I know," I said. "But I live a good distance from those mountains."

"Oh yes. America is very big! Ve-ry big! Alaska is very much bigger."

"Have you been to Alaska?" I asked.

"Oh yes. McKinley. I climbed McKinley. Very beautiful."

I believed he had. He wore gray cotton knickers, and I could see his calves, powerful looking and fuckin' huge.

Then the Wild Man said to Noguchi, "You Japanese?"

"Hai, sumimasen," Noguchi said.

"Polite guy," the Wild Man said to me.

Noguchi motioned me to the Wild Man's open fly. "His social window is open," he whispered to me.

A few days earlier, sitting at Mr. Donut in Kitami, I had noticed Noguchi's fly was down. I said, "Hey, your barn door is open." He looked at me quizzically. I said it again. He looked down, smiled, and pulled his zipper up.

"What?" he said. "Barn door? What?"

"Right," I said. "You know. Your cows and horses might get out."

He laughed loudly then. "We say: Your social window is open," he told me. And we both laughed at that. The Wild Man's open social window mattered little at the top of Iouzan, but Noguchi seemed concerned. He spoke to the Wild Man in Japanese: "Excuse me, I'm sorry, but you're social window is open. I'm so sorry."

The Wild Man looked down at himself. "Yes, of course," he said, as if wondering why we didn't have our flies open too. "Ventilation! Always like this." And then, "Most polite guy," he said of Noguchi. Then he said, "Let me tell you my name. And you will never forget it because of the bomb. My name is Hiroshi, from Fukushima. Maybe you know Hiroshima? Now you won't forget me. I am fifty-six years old. I speak six languages. French, you know. Of course Japanese. English. I am one of English instructor, you know. Greek. Latin. And something else." He paused. "Oh yes, Nepalese. Would you like to hear something?"

"Yes," I said. "Please."

"I give you Genesis in Latin!" and he belted out the opening verses of the Pentateuch.

"Beautiful," I said.

"Yes, of course," he said. "Very beautiful. Would you like to hear something else?"

"Not necessarily," I said.

"All right, then. I'll say something in Nepalese." And he did.

"You been to Nepal?" I asked him, trying to advance the conversation.

"Of course. Mountain climbing. What else? Eleven peaks in Himalayas. Six in Africa. Dozens in USA and Canada. And maybe everything in Japan. Maybe there are others. I've been out for ten days this trip, and this is peak number 12. Tomorrow I go to Rausu Mountain." He pointed into the distance with his ice axe, which he noticed me noticing.

"This is my weapon against the bear," he said. "Most people fear the bear, but my case is little different. I want to meet the bear, not run from him. I want to talk with the bear. So I come to the mountain alone." He paused. "Why are you here?"

I heard some gravity in his voice. He wasn't making small talk. Why was I here? His reason sounded simple enough, but then I realized that seeing (or talking to) a bear was much more to him than some big sexy megafauna he could add to his Cool Animals I Have Seen list. What he was saying was that instead of fearing bears, instead of running from them, he was walking out to meet them. I liked this idea, that stepping in to face potentially scary things feels better than running away from them. Maybe this was the missing piece in my life. Maybe this was why I had come. But I backed down.

"I'm just visiting," I said. "I used to live here in Hokkaido."

"Oh. English teacher?! Yes, many Americans do like that."

"Right," I said.

"Wrong," he said. "Tell me true. Why are you on top of this mountain? In the olden time, the sages climbed to top-of-the-mountain for solitude and meditation, fasting and praying. Why are you here?" Then he snatched my arm with his powerful hand, pulled it toward him, and began stroking me, "Nice arm! Oh, so nice arm!"

He really was crazy. And yet, his question urged me on. Why was I here? To relieve the boredom of an ordinary life? To recover from my divorce? To find myself? Put that way, a search for Self now seemed rather dull and ordinary, and restoration post-divorce sounded routine and all too American, maybe all too human. It was everyone's story, wasn't it? Maybe this was the Wild Man's story too.

"Nice climbing shoe," he said suddenly, looking down at my feet. "Maybe we trade? My boots are too old. Anyway," he said, "the mountain is my church. My religion. Before, I had no religion. I had no idea for my life. So I went up the mountain. I stood at the top, and my ego vanished. I became empty and ready to receive anything from the outside." He paused a moment, then said, "Our life is short. Eternity is long. We must enjoy our life."

His voice grew louder. More wild. "Here's what I think," he continued. "You want to know what I think? Yes, you do. Every human person must have some spirit. They must wake up. They must have a big feeling in their heart, and vanish the ego, like mine, or else we have too much war and sorrow. My life is simple here in the clouds."

He looked up. Noguchi and I looked up, too, and we *were* in the clouds. Dark and misty storm clouds had moved in around us.

"Ah, this is the mountain life," he said. "So easy and fast to change. This cloud means time to go," he said, and started down. We hurried down after him.

With the clouds converging overhead, the Wild Man moved swiftly, like a lizard, over the rocks, over the surface of the mountain, the huge, enduring, ungovernable mountain, and the distances running out across the earth's seas that surrounded us were beautiful, so beautiful and blue, blue, blue. I followed him, covering the ground as fast as I could, trying to keep up. I heard a soft giggling from the Wild Man, a soft giggling like water flowing over rock. He let the mountain set the pace under his legs, it was so much like play to him. Ah, I thought, here it is. This is why I've come. Just to meet the Wild Man, to shift that self-absorbed voice that rails and flounders and pleads: "Dear God! Why me? I am so brutalized by the world and deserve some comfort!" Meanwhile, the mountain goes on being the mountain. The sky, the sky. The clouds, the clouds. All of it, uncomplaining in any kind of weather. And how beautiful. How astonishing to recognize that this is so.

In the steepest place, clinging to the rocks, Noguchi's hands started shaking again. "Looks scared," the Wild Man said to Noguchi. "Don't worry. Just climb down. But no mistakes, please. Just one mistake in the mountain and that can be your last. This life is so simple, right? This way," he said, leading us on.

All the way down he talked out his life philosophy, saying over again what he had said, like he didn't want us to forget it. "The mountain is my religion," he said, and "My ego was vanished," and "You'll never forget my name," and "We have too much war." We came to the place he had stowed his pack. He hefted it onto his back.

"Here I leave you," he said. "You have e-mail? I'll visit to you in Wyoming. I'll climb the Tetons. They have bears too, right?"

He produced a scrap of paper and I wrote down my address. I didn't want him to go. I had only just awakened.

"So long," the Wild Man said, and he turned and walked on to the next peak.

Watanabe stood up as Noguchi and I approached from our summit climb. He welcomed us like heroes, like we had come home from a great journey. Excitedly we told him the story of the Wild Man, told him what the Wild Man had told us, described how he looked, demonstrated by opening our social windows and parading around. We laughed and laughed, and in that gift of laughter from the Wild Man I felt a lightness I had not felt in months.

With the clouds wheeling overhead we hurried with our lunch, and then packed up and started down the trail into the tangled pines. It was late afternoon when we reached the end, the trailhead where we had begun. I was exhausted. My legs wobbly. My stomach empty and happy. Bending to unlace my boots I noticed a sticker on the back of a Toyota Landcruiser parked near Noguchi's car. Characteristic of the way the Japanese use English, it read:

NORTH ISLAND, HOKKAIDO
It is only for moment spending
in the wilderness. But the memory
leaves forever. The river opened
up the road. Walk on it.

And so we had.

Mountains Belong to People Who Love Them

A mountain is also something in the body, not solely something the body is in. When the Chinese recluse poet Han Shan wrote, "Try and make it to Cold Mountain," his counsel was to travel to a place in the mind, or a place in the spirit, if you prefer. I think he means that one should pursue a life of spiritual practice, a practice that is a pilgrimage to the deep places inside the Self—on such a journey, what is hidden there may then be revealed. The journey to that place, which Han Shan calls Cold Mountain (indeed, Cold Mountain is an alternate name for Han Shan), begins as a descent, not as a climb—you go down, down, into the dark parts of the mind, into the unconscious, where the dragons live. These dragons are actually part of the Self. After doing battle with the dragons, after defeating them, you climb up and out. Somehow in this transformation of the Self, in the achievement of Self-mastery, that chasm you at first descended becomes a mountain, and you climb up it.

This is also Dante's story in the *Inferno*. He reaches the deepest level of Hell and finds Satan lodged in the ice, with Brutus, Cassius, and Judas forever flensed by the teeth of his three mouths. Dante wonders how he may get out of Hell, since this part of his journey is now complete. Instead of climbing back up the way they had gone down, Dante's guide, Virgil, instructs that they must go deeper still, past "the point / to which, from every part, all weights are drawn." Is this the unconscious? Beyond this point, the descent becomes an ascent, a summit bid. The poem reads:

My guide and I came on that hidden road
to make our way back into the bright world;
and with no care for any rest, we climbed—

The two travelers emerge to "see—once more—the stars."

There at the summit of Dante's journey is where we find ourselves in the final verses of Yeats's great poem "Lapis Lazuli." It is too easy to find darkness in this world. You look and you find it. You don't look, and you also find it. I have friends who have attempted to hide out from the world and its darknesses by taking refuge in the mountains. But the mountains encourage engagement with the world, not retreat. So this design always fails. To revise John Muir, going up is really going in. In fact, from the height of mountains the world's darkness is even clearer, more apparent, and on the mountaintop you are more exposed than ever. So here we come to Yeats.

The poem's achievement is in "Gaiety transfiguring all that dread." Look you here:

Those Chinamen climb towards, and I
Delight to imagine them seated there;
There, on the mountain and the sky,
On all the tragic scene they stare.
One asks for mournful melodies;
Accomplished fingers begin to play.
Their eyes mid many wrinkles, their eyes,
Their ancient, glittering eyes, are gay.

So the clearest view of the world is from the mountaintops, and looking down over the world at the tragic scene one must discover the capacity for acceptance. Suffering comes only from a resistance to an undeniable truth. Yeats gives us: "All things fall and are built again." There is harmony, however (the "mournful melodies") in the balance of falling and building. Gratefully, Yeats gives us one more line to affirm necessity and purpose:

And those that build them again are gay.

Here is not just a formula, but a task.

I was born in Fairbanks, Alaska, then spent the formative years of my life (age two to eighteen) in the Oregon Cascades, that beautiful volcanic range that flows south out of Washington, across Oregon, and into the Sierra. The forests over the western slopes of these mountains are moist and mossy and huge. The land comes up around you like a cradle, like that first cradle that protects the infant from tumbling onto the floor. It was a fine course of mountains to grow up in, or to have grow up in me.

After living in many different places in the west and overseas, I now make my home on the tablelands of the Texas panhandle, the Llano Estacado. The llano, according to a geographer I know, is one of the flattest landscapes on Earth. The highest point for some 300 miles north to south, and 150 miles east to west, is any of the several freeway overpasses on the loop highway encircling the sprawling city of Lubbock. One friend, a Texan who has lived here most of her life, has written about the llano as the "cotton-fucked ugliness of the plains." There is almost nothing immediately appealing about this place, and most of the people I know who live here desire most to leave.

But I tell you, even living on the Llano, I am a mountain person.

I'm sorry, but living in the mountains may not get the mountains into you. By my count, it is not simply a function of time. So, how will you do it? How will you absorb and be absorbed by the great peaks of the world? Can you create or demand a formative experience in the mountains, like childhood? (I make no special claims here—my childhood was an accident, like yours.) Perhaps you must climb mountains? Or undertake some other kind of journey through which toil, suffering, and fear makes you into a mountain? Don't just wait around your whole life paying property taxes in a hip ski town.

How about studying these three passages from Dogen's *Mountains and Waters Sutra*, taught to the assembly at Kannondōri Kōshō Hōrin Monastery at the hour of the Rat in the year 1240:

from 22
An ancient buddha said, "Mountains are mountains, waters are waters." These words do not mean mountains are mountains; they mean mountains are mountains.

from 17
Mountains have been the abode of great sages from the limitless past to the limitless present. Wise people and sages all have mountains as their inner chamber, as their body and mind. Because of wise people and sages, mountains appear.

from 18
Although mountains belong to the nation, mountains belong to people who love them.

Hunger at the Mountain

I

Camped in Death Valley near Furnace Creek in late December, I cannot imagine this place as a deep depression in the Earth's crust. Badwater, a few miles south of here, is 282 feet below sea level, the lowest point in North America. What I see instead are the Funeral Mountains rising sharply on the northeast side of the campground and, out across the wide valley to the southwest, the great Panamint Range, with 11,049-foot Telescope Peak. Nor does the temperature here this winter hold the promise of deadly summer sun. On July 10, 1913, Furnace Creek achieved the second highest recorded temperature on Earth: 134 degrees Fahrenheit. But at night in my tent I pull the drawstring of my down bag closed against the cold, leaving only a small hole for breathing. Instead of the deep sweltering bowl that is Death Valley, the vision before me could be any place high in the Andes or in the foothills of the Himalayas, a sharp wind funneling down from the snowy crags. Beyond this discrepancy, a single thought comes clear: this place I am in—one of Earth's lowest, hottest, driest, most inhospitable landscapes—is also one of the most beautiful places I've ever seen.

It was not easy to get here, and it will not be easy to get out. I have left my family and friends, left the excesses of holiday food and cheer and gift-giving, for one purpose: to complete the New Year's vision quest with the California-based School of Lost Borders. We are eight men and women who will go out into the desert to fast for four days and nights; two guides, Angelo Lazenka and Emerald North; and two assistant guides, Jennifer Yamamoto and Robert Wagner.

The vision quest (also called a "wilderness rite of passage") is an initiation ceremony by which one marks a major life change. A marriage for example, or a divorce. The death of a loved one, or a birth. The transition from childhood to adulthood, or from adulthood to elderhood. Marking such life changes is a vital part of many cultures, including native peoples in North America. But the vision quest at the school does not rely on any one tradition. It is a collage of traditions refined by the collective experience of the school's guides, and its founders, Steven Foster and Meredith Little. The vision quest under their tutelage consists of three stages: four days of preparation, known as "severance"; four days of fasting in a wild landscape alone, known as the "threshold"; and four days of group work to interpret and understand the threshold experience, known as "incorporation."

Severance (to break or separate) is both real and symbolic. A faster may use the vision quest to end a relationship with a person, a place, or a memory, for good. Or, in acknowledgement of the change a faster will undergo during the vision quest, they symbolically sever all bonds with their former life and former Self. The person who departs for a quest will not be the same person who returns. This stage often begins long before arrival at the fasting place, months before, sometimes even years.

Another key aspect of severance is the formation of a personal intention. Counter to the popular notion that a vision quest evokes a mystical experience or an encounter with a spiritual realm, Foster and Little assert in their book, *The Book of the Vision Quest*, that "You must be very clear with yourself about why you are leaving everything behind and going alone and hungry upon the Earth." This clarity, usually formed into a statement, guides the faster to his vision. It does not come magically. Foster and Little write, "You would have to *want* to change and then go about doing whatever was necessary to secure those changes." Embarking on a vision quest means undertaking hard work.

And what is a vision? According to Angelo Lazenka, "it's the naming and claiming of what an individual already knows is the gift they have to offer the world. It's as simple as that," he said. "There's a sense in me that as we move through our lives, we can uncover or excavate deeper and deeper the gifts we already possess. I think rites of passage are a way to really honor the necessity to die to everything that wasn't serving, or needed to fall away. It's that last excavation or uncovering so you can see what gifts you have to bring to your community, family, people, and culture." In this regard, then, there is no flash of light or ray of wisdom from heaven. The faster goes out alone with an intention, and returns to the world to make good on it.

The threshold stage is the time alone without food in nature. What happens out there is between you and the wild land. You take only the bare minimum to survive: a sleeping bag and a shelter (tarp or tent), one gallon of water for each day, warm clothing, a journal perhaps. You go out and sit alone upon the Earth. You leave behind your many life roles: parent, employee, friend, sibling, taxpayer, citizen. You face no thing and no one but yourself. You are, perhaps for the first time since you were born, nothing more than a human being.

The incorporation stage is the rest of your life. In the short term, each faster returns from the threshold to tell his story to the guides and the rest of the group. The guides help to interpret and validate the story in a process called "mirroring." The faster then takes his story and returns home, knowing that its meaning and his understanding of it will shift and deepen, probably for years.

These three stages of the vision quest ceremony mirror the three stages of the mythic hero's journey: departure, passage, and arrival. The passage of the mythic hero is a physical journey to be sure, an outward one, but it is also fundamentally inward. When the hero makes his descent into the underworld (remember Beowulf enters the lair of Grendel's mother) he is also making a descent into the unconscious, the part of himself where all his fears and secrets are hidden. He must do battle with these fears and secrets (his demons and monsters) and, in overcoming them, ascend to the surface with new powers and wisdom. "If only a portion of that lost totality could be dredged up into the light of day," writes Joseph Campbell in *The Hero with a Thousand Faces*, "we should experience a marvelous expansion of our powers, a vivid renewal of life. We should tower in stature." Furthermore, the "lost totality" the hero dredges up is not only valuable to himself but also to his "whole generation or [his] entire civilization." The hero defeats his demons and claims power for himself, and then offers this power as a gift to his people. In so doing he shows them the way to their own power. This is what Lazenka meant when he said that a vision is "the naming and claiming of what an individual already knows is the gift they have to offer the world." The idea of "gift implies that it was not yours to begin with. It was gifted to you. Your attributes, your qualities, your passions were given to you. And you need to give them back."

At its sharpest edge, the vision quest is a ceremony for learning how to die. You go out into the empty land and a part of you dies, the part that is not needed anymore. You return fully alive as your new self. But a symbolic death can come very close to a real death—it is dangerous out there in the wild. And you are alone. You come face to face with this unshakeable truth: you will, one day, die. This truth is necessary, because, as Campbell writes, "In the United States there is even a pathos of inverted emphasis: the goal is not to grow old, but to remain young; not to mature away from Mother, but to cleave to her." This heraldry of youth is a kind of illness because it leads to the illusion of immortality. The only way beyond it is to acknowledge and accept the darkness that lies at the limits of the unconscious, to know in the mind and in the body that this world, as Campbell writes, "yields but one ending: death, disintegration, dismemberment, and the crucifixion of our heart with the passing of the forms that we have loved." This knowing is the inheritance of all who pass from childhood to adulthood—we are born out of the bliss of the womb and into the sorrow of the tomb. Emerald North, the other guide I worked with, names this place "the plains of sadness." The only way to live unshackled by the plains of sadness is to make an inward journey there and look around for a time. There is nothing to do with it. There is no way to get rid of it. Merely facing the darkness of oblivion offers surprising renewal and the release of one's gifts. "When our day is come for the victory of death," writes Campbell, "death closes in; there is nothing we can do, except be crucified—and resurrected; dismembered totally, and then reborn."

A hero, then, is a man or a woman who is able to "die to the past and be reborn to the future," as Campbell writes, someone who is able to change, to mindfully make the transition to each new stage of life. To go on a vision quest is to become a hero.

During my short stay over the holidays at my parents' home in southwest Idaho, family and friends asked me questions about the vision quest. It wasn't easy to explain myself, partly because I wasn't sure why I was going. I'm not a champion of therapy and I don't take readily to feel-good group work. In fact, I avoid both. When everyone is hugging and exclaiming their loyalty and love after a dinner party, I'm the one standing outside on the front walk, eager for solitude and fresh air. I'm a skeptic, generally, and at my worst that attitude can rise into dismissal and contempt for other people's beliefs. With these admissions it's a wonder I made it to Death Valley at all. Yet I know that such skepticism can be a cover for weakness or unfulfilled desires. Hidden here is my admiration for people who live a spiritual life, and I want such a life for myself. Out there in the desert, then, is the purest experience, a personal encounter with whatever is or is not in the wild. A personal encounter with god. But how does one explain this to friends and family?

Another complication in answering the question "why?" is that guided vision quests are expensive. The School of Lost Borders asks for a fee of between seven and twelve hundred dollars (you pay what you can, between those sums), and on top of that you pay for travel, camping, and food before and after the fast. You must bring all your own camping gear. It's hard to understand paying this kind of money and getting nothing tangible in return, not even a decent meal.

Some of the questions I heard were invitations, and allowed me to talk for upward of an hour about what I thought I was about to do. Other questions were aggressive and judgmental: "That's a lot of money to sit in the desert and not eat. Why can't you just go sit in your backyard?" or "Aren't you already a man?" or "So after you've found yourself, what then?"

Other fasters in my group reported similar experiences. When Angela Ramseyer told her mother about her plans to go on a vision quest, the response was: "And you won't be able to shower for how many days?" Pamela Stones, who has completed nine vision quests, told me she talks to very few people about her experiences. The term "desert retreat" is usually enough to satisfy most people she knows. Diann Hamant said a close relative told her that he'd be happy to lock her in his basement for four days without food and only charge her half as much. Inevitably, any interrogation becomes part of the severance stage, a small challenge that calls up the faster's resolve and echoes the big test ahead in the wild.

II

We position our chairs in a circle away from view of the busy Texas Springs campground. The place is a shallow depression in sun-seared soils devoid of vegetation, a mirror of greater Death Valley. The place seems made for us, made for this purpose, to sit together and talk plainly of real things.

Already the group feels easy with itself, our bond forming fast around our common purpose. We sit in council, passing a smudge bowl, while Emerald breaks the clear morning with her rough laughter. Three ravens come in, circling our circle, and cruise off with a raucous caw-caw-caw. Emerald watches them go. "The raven thinks so," she announces. This establishes a tone for us, for the way in which we will speak to each other—the exterior landscape and its creatures are an inseparable part of the interior landscape, the landscape of the spirit and the heart. It isn't important to ask science if this is so. We do not deprecate this agreement with trust or distrust in New Age ideals. None of us is truly or falsely holy. We are merely human beings who feel something that is hard to pull down into language when the ravens pass. "I just have to make sure you know," assistant guide Jennifer Yamamoto told me one evening, "I have no special powers or knowledge."

For the next several days, each faster will work out the terms of his or her intention. The process takes about one hour per person. The faster begins by talking about what led him to the circle. In some cases the impetus is clear. In other cases the guides must tease out an intention that the faster is unable to articulate. It helps that some members of the group have fasted before. What each of us is left with is a single statement that we may copy into our notebooks and hold in mind during the threshold time. The intention becomes a companion as well as a goal. Without it, the fast might be meaningless.

I do not have permission to tell anyone else's story. So I will tell my own.

I wait until the third day. I am not eager to talk about myself. I don't wish for anyone to uncover my weaknesses. Knowing that I'll be asked for a statement of intention, I have prepared one: "I am home." Maybe the statement will be enough, and I won't have to say much more. But no. I begin by telling the group that I want to reclaim a sense of home. That I feel lost. I wonder if I belong on Earth. I'm not suicidal. I mean that I don't feel connected or grounded. I recently went through a divorce, and ironically it was my ex-wife, an equine-assisted therapist, who introduced me to the possibility of a vision quest. I think I don't want children. I've spent my whole life moving from place to place, and most recently moved from a place I had grown to love in southeast Wyoming to a place I'm unsure about in west Texas. My new job teaching nature writing and literature in the Honors College at Texas Tech University is a fine career move. But I feel hypocritical: How can I lead students to discover a sense of place when I feel so out of place myself? Shouldn't I have chosen a home over a job? These are not original troubles, but this feeling has become a kind of crisis in my daily life because I acknowledge that if I don't belong here on Earth, I don't belong anywhere.

Angelo and Emerald encouraged me to broaden my statement, to make it more specific. It becomes: "I am a warm, trustworthy, enduring, steadfast, loving man at home on Earth." Although I hear murmurs of approval when I say it back to the group, I do not like my statement. It feels precious, too self-help-ish, too exposed. I don't like reporting it to you here, although without it, my experience during the fast might be meaningless.

One more story is necessary if you are to follow my experience during the threshold time. Working out my intention in the group, a long pause went between me and my guides. I didn't plan to tell this story. It made its presence in my mind, and I began to speak.

In the fall of 2002, in southeast Wyoming, I went out walking behind my rented house on the Wyoming Hereford Ranch. I could see for miles, all the way to the wind generators lining Interstate 25 near Colorado. The sun was going down, and the wind was cold and sharp against my face. Angling down into a draw, I saw a jumble of feathers on the ground. Some great bird must have died there, and now, after being ravaged by coyotes, the feathers shuddered in the wind. As I neared the place where it was, I could see that the bird looked like a hawk, a red-tailed hawk, lying on its back. I could see the shape of the head turned toward me, the sharp beak, and the wings and tail feathers curved up into the shape of a bowl. As I approached, the dead thing transformed into something alive; the bird opened its mouth, exposing the hollow of its throat and its tongue. It looked straight at me. I heard a gurgling sound from the hawk like it could not breathe. Then I noticed something wound around the hawk, something binding it up around the middle and across its legs.

I picked up a small stone and jabbed the thing with the point of it. It uncoiled then and became a snake, reared its head at me, and struck twice as I took my hand back. A bull snake, I thought, a constrictor, not venomous. Should I leave now, let things go on as they had, or should I intervene? Then something rose up inside me, an angry desire to rescue the hawk, to save it, to save its beauty perhaps.

I searched the ground for something to poke at the snake, but there was nothing. No trees or shrubs or anything to make a branch, nothing but grass and rock and sky. I hurried up the slope toward the fence searching the ground, and then I found it, a long length of shiny flat metal. I took it up like a sword, and carried it back. I reached in with the weapon and marked the snake on the back, cut it, and excited it, and it reared up against me and struck at me, and I struck back. It paused, ready with its mouth open for another attack, the soft wet pink of its throat exposed. I stuck the metal between its jaws and twisted it, and the snake recoiled, and I felt my heart racing, my hands shaking, and I did it again, and then I rapped it hard on the head, and the snake seemed to tighten its grip as the hawk's eyes went wide and terror lived there, and then the snake fell, and rolled a little, and relaxed, and released. I moved to the side where its head lay on the Earth, and I chopped at it and missed and hit the hawk in the wing. I met the hawk's eyes again with mine and I struck again, and I heard a high-pitched PING! that was the end of the length of metal breaking off and laying over there as the rest of it cut the snake's head, and blood moved out of it. The snake went limp in the body now, and I lifted it with my weapon, and pulled it away from the hawk and cast it to the side. It writhed and rolled and looked alive, and I picked up a heavy stone and smashed it down on the snake's head and crushed it and left it there where it lay like a rope.

I sat crouched on my hams, my heart racing and cooling, the weapon still in my grip. I had not intended to kill the snake. But I did. And now I wanted something in return. I wanted the hawk to fly off. It didn't. It lay there like before, as if nothing had changed, as if the snake were still around it. As if I had not made a sacrifice to save it.

I reached in, mindful of the talons and of the sharp, hooked beak, and gathered the tail feathers like flowers in my hand. I pulled the hawk toward me, dragging it across the dry ground as it opened its mouth wider, its eyes were giant Os. Still it did not or could not get up. I went around behind it, crouched there as it turned its head almost all the way around, and I touched its powerful wings, pulled them out gently, and stroked them and pressed them in, testing the muscles and bones. When I released them, they remained there, jutting straight up into the air.

If the hawk remained here into the night something would come along, a coyote probably, and carry it off. My only other option was to carry it off myself. I had entangled myself in the hawk's story this far, so why not take it to someone out there who could heal it? Or would it recover better on its own? Would moving it kill it? I felt both obligations at once: to leave it and to take it with me. I waited. Evening fell.

I stood and walked home in the dark.

The next morning I went back to the place. A hard frost covered over the plain, and it sparkled in the sun. The hawk was gone. Not even a feather remained. The snake was a string of bloody bones. Something had eaten it in the night. My weapon lay where I had left it. I lingered only a moment, and then turned and walked back up the draw. Ahead of me I saw a hawk perched on a fence post. The moment was somehow unremarkable, as if the hawk had always been there, maybe watching me. As I drew near, the hawk lifted off and flew over my head and back behind the hills.

. . .

After I told this story in the circle, Angelo said that I had saved the hawk, something I have never believed. He also said that the hawk, now freed, had devoured the snake that held it captive. "You have released yourself from the thing that binds you," Angelo said to me. "Not only that, but you have eaten of that thing, consumed its power over you."

Emerald said, "You have been so hungry for spirit! Now you must go out on your fast and become spirit."

III

December 31, 2005—15 hours without food

There is absolutely nothing I must do. I am camped alone on a high flat up Hanaupah Canyon on the west side of Death Valley. The flat is one hundred feet off the canyon floor. Out in front of me is the edge that drops straight down. I'm tucked back against the mountainside. We spent the previous day finding our solo sites and packing out our four one-gallon bottles of water from base camp. I walked to the limit of safety, about one hour, a distance of time established by the school. I wanted to get as close as possible to the base of Telescope Peak, which towers over me but is now shrouded in purple rain clouds. It occurred to me, on that walk, that I was wasting time trying to make distance when instead I should have been searching for the best site to camp. Headed up the side canyon to where my place is now, I discovered a fragile eggshell near the toe of my boot. Inside, the yellowed membrane curled away from the smooth interior. It might be a chukar egg, I thought. I saw a group of chukars on my way up the canyon. Of course, I also thought of the hawk and snake. Because the vision quest is a self-made ceremony (no one is here to interpret anything for me), I decided the eggshell meant that I was on the right path. I climbed up onto the flat, left my water next to a creosote bush, and placed the eggshell there too, in an outcropping of dry grass. I am seated beside it, the eggshell, seated in my Thermarest chair, my journal in my lap, my black skullcap pulled down around my ears as the temperature drops with the clouds that now begin to spend their rain.

I retreat to my tent. The rain freshens the dry air. It smells so good. It's raining hard now, slamming against my rain fly. Not everyone took a tent along. A tarp is usually the only shelter a faster uses. I weighed the situation, however—down sleeping bag, no food, and a forecast of rain, wind, and cold. I'll only use the tent to keep dry, I counsel myself. I'm not cheating.

Inside, I sit in my chair and make notes in my journal. I take my time. There is nothing else for me to do. I use the few colored pencils I brought along to draw a diagram of my buddy circle, the circle of stones down canyon where another faster and I will leave a marker each day to indicate that we are all right. I go each morning; she goes each afternoon. I finish my drawing and, feeling bored and restless, I lie down and pull my loose sleeping bag over me.

Sometime later I wake up, but I don't know how much later or what time of day it is. I unzip the rain fly and look out at the gray sky so close to the Earth. It's still raining. I zip the rain fly down. I lie there shivering for a time. I think maybe I should heat some water on my backpacking stove. Drink something. But I don't bother. I make a few more notes in my journal, listening to the rain. I have nothing to do. Emerald's words come into my head. Seated at the fire at Texas Springs she began to laugh in the loud, smoker's way that she cackles, and she said, "You're all going to be sitting out there soon, in the desert alone. And there's NOTHING out there!"

The poem I copied into the back of my journal follows her words, Wallace Stevens's "The Snowman." I don't need to read it. It's lodged in my memory, especially the last two lines:

And, nothing himself, beholds
Nothing that is not there and the nothing that is.

Soon I'm waking up again. I can't remember falling asleep. It's dark now, and the sky is clear. The day has passed me by. Stars wheel overhead. Billions and billions of stars. I can see Orion and the Big Dipper. A falling star crashes through the night. Something else moving slowly, a plane, maybe. A plane probably. It's cold, but I crawl out anyway and pull on my heavy fleece anorak. I sit in my chair and fire up my stove, a tiny blue flame in all this blackness. The hot water warms me from the inside, and I feel suddenly happy and content. I heat more water and watch the blue flame die away. I hear an owl across the canyon. It's probably a great horned owl, but I'll never know.

I pull my sleeping bag out of the tent, lay it out on my sleeping pad and climb in. I lie there under the great sky, the fabulous stars, and after some time, an hour maybe, three hours, I don't know, I fall asleep.

January 1, 2006—40 hours without food

I wake in darkness. The night is fourteen hours long, and it's still night, but I think it's also the next day. Diann Hamant gave each of us a sparkler to ring in the New Year. I remember mine and fetch it out of the side pocket in my tent. To the east, lightning pulses above the Amargosa Range. I stand there on the edge of the canyon, light the sparkler, and say good morning and Happy New Year to each of the people in my group, the fasters and the guides at base camp. Then I call out the names of all the people in my family, and a few friends. "Happy New Year!" I say to them.

The sparkler dies and I'm cold again. I get into my sleeping bag and sit up in my chair. I heat more water and drop in an herbal tea bag. I think soon the sun will rise. It doesn't. I sleep again.

In the morning I think of breakfast. My stomach is empty and angry. I pour a packet of electrolyte replacement powder into my water and drink it. This is an optional supplement the guides offered us before departure. Since I have to cross a long flow of boulders on the far end of the flat to get to the buddy pile, I think it's better not to feel dizzy. I stand up. I feel dizzy. I sit down. I notice the egg shell there at the base of the creosote. How did it weather all that wind and rain of yesterday? I watch the morning bloom.

The sky is cast in clouds, and darker heavier clouds pester me to the west against the mountain. I decide that after I visit the buddy pile I'll walk up canyon. Robert Wagner told me that when he fasted here a year ago, he walked up to the snow line. And there's an old mine shaft up there to see. And water runs in the creek bed. The more I walk, I figure, the less idle time I'll have. The less time I'll have to feel lonely. The less time I'll have to feel hungry, to think of food. A human being can go for weeks without food, months even. Four days is nothing. Besides, this hunger in my belly isn't about food. That's what Angelo told me anyway. That's what I read in Foster and Little's book. This is a spiritual hunger. I nod to it, wishing I had a great big omelet with bacon. I fill my water bottle and strap on my waist pack with a first aid kit inside.

At the buddy pile I find that my buddy, Cait Cain, has left an indistinct stone on top of my large diamond-shaped stone. All is well. I head out. After the long night I'm happy to be walking a good pace and soon I'm sweating lightly. The canyon is open and easy and I follow the two-track road up to its end. It takes me a couple of hours, walking slowly with my empty belly. Clouds swirl overhead covering and releasing the sun. The mountain reveals itself and towers over me. It is so vivid in fresh snow I can hardly look at it.

It looks like the canyon ends here, but it turns sharply to the north. I sit down at this junction and drink water from my bottle. I could go back, I think, or I could go on. I don't know.

I go on.

Around that bend in the canyon a few little brown birds draw my sense. I stand with my back to a sheer rock face, facing the brush on the other side. The little birds move as one. I watch them. Each movement seems a vivid display. Behind me I hear wings, probably a raven. The ravens are everywhere in Death Valley, and the sound of their wings is almost as loud as their voice. It could be the owl, I suppose, but not likely. I hear the wings again. I turn around, and nothing is there.

Then the nothing becomes something, and I know this just before I see it, the wings spread wide and the body hung beneath them, wide and rock-colored. The hawk falls and cruises that short distance to another perch on the cliffside, its red tail flaring like a fan to balance it. I stand there looking at this hawk. I hear myself talking to it as if I've already said what I'm saying, and now I'm listening from some other place. I don't know what I say. Some kind of request, or I plead a question, or I pray. I can see into the hawk's black eyes. They go all the way back to the Big Bang. And I can see its hooked beak, the killing force behind it, and then the mouth opens, the tongue a sharp dart inside, as the hawk screams at me. A little tremor goes up my back. I wait inside the echo and the hawk screams again and drops from its place in the rock, turns the canyon corner, and leads me away.

I follow it. Moments later there is no hawk to follow but I keep going, all the way back to my place, up the game trail to my tent and sleeping bag. I sit down. I record what I've just seen in my journal, to make it real. I try to explain it. This hawk is mere coincidence, I think. The red tail is one of the most widely distributed hawks in North America, so if I am to see a hawk, it's likely to be a red tail. But I'm on the other side of my doubt now, and I can't deny my belief in this hawk, that it came from some other place, that it came to speak to me.

Some hours pass. The clouds come in like anger and force me into my tent. I lie in there shivering until I pull my sleeping bag on like a pair of pants. The wind comes up in the heavy rain and challenges the huge rocks I've used to tie out the corners of the tent and rain fly. One great gust comes in and fouls everything. I go out to secure the tent again. It's cold and the rain stings my hands. I finish and dive into the tent, wrap up in my down bag, pull my skullcap down over my ears. It goes on like this for hours. It gets darker and darker until I fall away into morning.

January 2, 2006—65 hours without food

The vision quest tradition is not a peyote trip, the Native American ceremonial hallucinogen that so many New Age hippies seek out as an excuse for getting high. Nor does the quest utilize acid or LSD or the Amazonian spirit drug ayahuasca. There is nothing going on here but fasting in a wild land. I repeat this to myself because when I wake to the dawn, I wonder if the hawk was real. I wonder if people will believe me when I tell my story in the circle. Will people regard me as an attention-seeking liar who knows that there is no one here to dispute what I invent?

The hawk is real.

The sky is awash in dark clouds, which cluster meanly along the mountaintops. When the rain breaks I make the trek down to the buddy pile. I feel weak and light-headed most of the way. It takes me a long time to cross the boulder field, I walk so carefully. Cait delights me by leaving a piece of Mylar balloon battered by the desert. "LOVE" is printed in purple letters. To tell her I'm alive I place a white stone that looks like a canine skull.

I have a job to do back at my place. Angelo and Emerald suggested that each of us make a "purpose circle," a ring of stones which we will try to sit inside from dusk to dawn on the last night and pray for a vision.

Since part of my intention is about claiming home, Angelo suggested the circle is essential to my ceremony. "Experiment by sitting on the outside of the circle, and then jump inside and claim it," he told me. This is a self-made ceremony. It doesn't follow any tradition. The faster goes into the wild and invents a way to talk to god. I don't know why I've not accomplished this task yet. I have all the time in the world to make my circle. I keep avoiding it. The only flat place to make it is where I put my tent, which again I crawl into to escape the rain.

The wind comes up and shakes me, rattles the rain fly and unsettles my heart. I want sun and warmth and an easy life. I want food and beer and coffee. I spent three months weaning myself off caffeine to make this trip. For what? I feel a growing disappointment and frustration, an awareness of the obvious stupidity of my situation. It's dark outside and inside the tent. The day is becoming one long night. I hear Jennifer Yamamoto's words in my head: "The payoff is measureless."

I lie on my back with the tent door open and the rain fly vestibule closed. The wind kicks up the dry earth beneath the fly and drops it over my face. I smell earth. I taste it. The wind surges violently, lifting the edge of the tent. I reach up with both hands and hold onto the tent pole that runs up over me in an arc. The wind slams me, and I grip tighter. This goes on far too long, I don't know how long, until the wind lightens, the rain stops, and I crawl out into the evening.

The mountain is somewhere behind the clouds. I stand there staring at it. I can't take my eyes off it. I can't help but think it doesn't want me here.

I make tea and sit in my chair. I have nothing to do. I think about my purpose circle and decide I'll use the break in the weather and the remaining light to work on it. But I just sit there. The clouds are flying by the mountain and it looks out at me, dressed in new snow, then disappears again as the clouds drop down, drop down, and cover everything.

"Break up! Leave me!" I shout at the storm. I don't make a habit of talking to mountains or weather, but this comes out of my mouth without my consent.

The first hard drops touch the rain fly. I sit in the rain for awhile. The wind hits me hard, and I realize I'm the best anchor my tent has. I crawl in, shed my outer layer of clothes, and get into my sleeping bag. I don't plan to get out until morning. The wind hits me so hard the tent fills with air like a kite. I kick one leg out of the bag and assume the position. My legs spread eagle, my hands stabilizing the arc of the tent. It's dark now. I hang on with each burst of the mountain's breath. This goes on and on in the darkness, my hands exposed and freezing in the winter air.

The wind slams me hard and the tent lifts up, folding me in it, then releases. I hold fast to the tent pole to keep it down, to keep it from taking off. The wind slams me. I yell out and hold on. It slams me. "YOU CAN'T PUSH ME OFF THIS MOUNTAIN!" I yell. I don't know where the words come from. I yell it again. The wind hits me. I yell it again, then again and again at the mountain. The tears come down. I realize I am in danger. I have to get out of this tent before the wind rolls me up in it and drives me over the ledge, that 100-foot drop off the flat. I hear Emerald's voice in my head: "Oh yes!" she says. "You could die out there." I'm holding and yelling, laying on my back on the cold ground, starving to death, a poor, weak, nameless animal yelling out at the mountain and the darkness that wraps me.

Some new part of me springs to life. *Think! Think!* I say to myself. I have to get out of this tent. I have to bring this tent down. I have to get my clothes on, my warm fleece and raincoat, my pants and boots. I can't go running off into the night in my underwear. I hold on to the tent with one hand, find my clothes in the darkness, get my pants on, somehow, I don't know how, stuff everything else under me, and sit up with both hands now on the tent poles in the wind, raging. The wind hits me and presses the tent into itself. I unzip the rain fly and there! The sky is brilliantly clear and so beautiful. It stops me a moment. I see the wind running like horses up the mountainside. I latch onto the tent poles and pull down on everything, bring the whole tent down around me and break out of the hole.

Suddenly I'm on top of the tent and everything is all right. The wind flows around me, but it can't move me or the tent or anything inside it. I take my time. I don't know what to do or where I'm going or how I'll get there. I just start packing up. I reach back inside the folded fabric and root around for my headlight. I put it on and turn it on. I'm meticulous about everything. I find my backpack inside the tent. Everything goes into it, ordered in the way it came out. I put my boots on. I pull the poles out of the collapsed folds, fold them, and put them into the stuff sack. The tent goes in after it. I wad it up and shove it in a little at a time.

I'm done with this place. There's nothing left for me here. I heft up my backpack, buckle the waist belt, and head down the flat. I don't know where I'm going. I keep as close to the mountainside as I can because I don't know how far it is the edge, that long drop from the flat to the canyon bottom. My light doesn't beam very far. I stumble because I'm walking too fast, it's night, I've not eaten in days, and the wind is whipping me in the back. I stumble and go down on my knees. I get up. I walk on a few paces and the wind knocks me down again. I get up. A creosote bush comes up out of the darkness. I step behind it into a depression in the ground and sit down.

Sheltered from the wind, I rest a little. I feel safe here. I sit. I think about nothing. I slump down, leaning in against my pack. Without warning the wind stops. It's still and quiet and the sky is a beautiful stillness of stars. An hour goes by. Maybe two. I feel calm again. Tired now. My eyes are heavy. There is no reason to sit here like this all night. I line the depression in the ground with my tarp, inflate my sleeping pad, roll out my bag, and climb in wearing all my clothes. The ground accepts my body right away. I fit perfectly in this little crevice. I look up at the starry, starry night. I think of nothing. I sleep until the sun breaks open the next day.

January 3, 2006—90 hours without food

Glorious morning. I wake to the sun-strike at the top of the canyon rim. I lay there in the crevice for a long time, the sun edge moving down, lighting everything. For the first time in many hours I feel hungry. Not empty, but the kind of hunger that comes when you're happy. I think of how close I am to food and friends. I have this day, the night, and then in the morning I'll pack up and walk into base camp. I feel like I've done it. But I'm not ready to go yet. I have work to do.

I put on my boots and walk back up the flat to retrieve my water jugs. About a hundred yards from the place I abandoned in the night I find two of the empty gallon jugs lodged under a creosote. They must have taken off in the wind, despite the heavy rocks I'd placed on top of them. I pick them up and walk on. There are my full gallon jugs of water where they should be, and beside them, the eggshell, just where I put it four days ago. I stare at it for awhile. It seems not possible. How did it hold its place in that wind? Do I leave it, or take it with me?

I take it with me.

In my new place near the crevice the day unfolds before me. I strip down in the warm sun and lay my clothes out on the ground. I lay my sleeping bag out too. I build my purpose circle. Inside the stone ring, I spread my tarp out where I will sleep this night. I've borrowed a rattle from Angelo, and I set that down inside the circle. I find dry grass beneath a cluster of creosote, gather up just enough, and form it into a nest. I set the egg shell inside, and set it near the rattle. A friend has given me some sweetgrass to burn. I place that in the circle.

Night arrives. The sky is mostly clear and promising. I feel whole again, like the storm tore me apart and the sun put me back together. But there will be no magic when I return. I will not be divinely transformed to feel at home. I must create a sense of belonging in the world. My intention for this vision quest, I realize, is not a list of how to be, but a list of what to do.

I get into my sleeping bag and sit up in my chair inside the circle. I rattle the rattle, making a nice rhythm in the dark. I say good-night and thank you to the other fasters, to the people at base camp, to my family and friends, to people long gone. It feels good to say thank you and call out their names to the mountain. It's all very simple and quiet. Time goes on so slowly I can't sense it anymore.

I put the rattle down. I'm tired and easy. I hear Angelo's voice: "If you fall asleep, you fall asleep." I decide I'll fall asleep. But not here. I get up and put my bed down in the crevice that saved me. The shape of the Earth here is the shape of my body. I sleep.

January 4, 2006—108 hours without food

Day breaks. I disassemble my purpose circle, as I will the buddy pile, to leave no mark of me behind. This eggshell came from here, so I leave it here. I shoulder my pack and walk in.

Not far from base camp I hear the drum. It awakens something inside me. I feel it in my heart, my throat, my mouth. The guides and one other faster who has come in before me wait at the threshold circle.

The drum gentles me in. Angelo says, "When you are ready to take on all that you've been given, step into the circle."

I step in.

Robert and Emerald bathe me in sage smoke. I close my eyes. I hear Emerald's voice, quiet now and so beautiful. She brushes me with feathers and fans the smoke over me, speaking to me, a whispering voice that I hear in front, behind, to the side. The sun is warm and the mountain is friendly at last. Her voice, her words become smoke and I drift away with them and then return as the smoke becomes words again with the drum tone that rises into a final strike when I hear Emerald say, "This-man who-has-come HOME!"

IV

"Mirroring" is the process by which the faster comes to understand his story from the threshold time. The faster tells his story in the circle, the guides retell the story they have just heard. It's that simple. The story's meaning is already there, and the guides illuminate it. "[The vision quest] has so little to do with the guide," Angelo told me, "and so much to do with the person. It's really focused on the faster. That's why Steven [Foster] used consciously the metaphor of midwife. A midwife supports this birthing, but does not try to change or fix anyone. The guide is a part of it, but not the focus of it. And I think that's essential to the work. It's why I keep doing the work. Because it's not about me."

The guides mirror in their own ways, using their particular strengths. The process can be like a conversation, or it can be like getting a talking- to, or it can be like theater. Emerald often uses song—it seems she knows a song to sing for every occasion, for every story—and she uses her powerful voice, she drives her voice directly into the faster's body like a medicine forcibly swallowed. Her eyes penetrate, too. She will stand, walk across the circle, and take something the faster is holding (a drum and an apple, in one case), and use that instrument as a tool in mirroring. She is inescapable, and everywhere at once in the story, drawing the disparate pieces she has just heard and assembling them into a beautiful whole. As forceful as she is, she is also nurturing. She cradles the story as if it were a baby to be loved.

Angelo can be as forceful as Emerald, but he seems to rely on a quieter retelling, the way an actor on stage can hush an audience by speaking softly. He sits with his eyes closed while someone else is mirroring, seemingly to take in the voices, the words without the clutter of visual signals. In his turn, he might ask himself a question aloud: "What is present for me now?" I heard him say this many times, and then answer that question in the mirroring. The question is a cue, a reminder that to mirror a faster's story is to embody it spontaneously, to animate it, to become the story for a brief time the way an actor becomes a character. Angelo often calls up related experiences from the days preceding the fast, or reminds the faster of something said casually around the fire one evening. The story does not begin and end with the threshold time. The faster is always living his story, always working with the same set of questions and tensions. Angelo discovers these points of contention and allows that the threshold experience is a microcosm of everyday life. Being in Angelo's presence is to be seen and acknowledged. Every word he speaks is a validation of one's humanity—yours and his.

The group—the guides and fasters—is essential to this process. We witness each other's story to make it real. And each of us sees a piece of our own story in everyone else's story. The stories then belong to the group, as well as the individual. By the end of this process I feel like I have known these people all my life.

Mirroring is just the beginning of this third "incorporation" stage of the vision quest. It is an entrance from the threshold to the rest of your life. "Soon you will realize," Foster and Little write, "that the only way to communicate the experience is not to talk about the vision but to live it." This is what fasting for four days in the wild is all about. The terms of your intention have not been met by fasting alone. The vision is only a glimpse of what is possible. The hard part is yet to come. "Your birth into the secular body of the modern world," they write, "is the most difficult step you will take in the entire vision quest rite."

I told my story in the circle. First Jennifer, then Angelo, and finally Emerald mirrored me. The process took about forty-five minutes.

"This is a man who during the storm speaks back to it," Jennifer said. Then she screamed my words out: "YOU CAN'T PUSH ME OFF THIS MOUNTAIN! YOU CAN'T PUSH ME OFF THIS MOUNTAIN!" She screamed it so loud and fiercely. That was me in the storm, I knew, and the storm returned to me again. The voice entered my bones, my heart and lungs, my blood. She loved where I had placed my tent, she said, in the only place I could build my purpose circle, that this move was the staking of my claim: "I belong here!" Jennifer said. "I belong here! I belong here!" The egg, she said, that was the place I had been, and I broke out of that egg, broke free of that shell of myself, and was reborn. "Oh yes," she said. "You died out there. And now you are home in every place you are."

Angelo stood up. He walked around the circle, put his hand on my shoulder, and continued around and around. This was me, is me, looking for a place to land, looking for a home. He walked the circle talking to me. "You saved the hawk," he said, "and it returned to save you." And then, "Men have been hanging onto the side of the mountain for a long time. They had to. They had to provide. Feed their families. Fight wars. Whatever. But that isn't working anymore . . . I honor you for bringing it down. Bringing it all down around you in the storm—the house, your life, the paradigm—for coming out through the hole, out through the tent. You were reborn. And birthing isn't easy. Being born is not easy . . . you did endure," he said. "With the consent of the mountain. The consent of the land. You stayed . . . I hope for one thing: that this experience comes so powerfully through your life that you can no longer deny the presence of spirit, the power of spirit that calls to you."

Emerald sang to me: "I'm go-ing up to the mountain, and I'm not com-ing down 'til morn-ning. I'm go-ing up to the mountain, and I'm not com-ing down 'til morn-ning." And from there I don't have specific words, but an experience of being inside Emerald's voice, her words as notes swarming around me and I sat in the middle of them, powerful and grave and ugly, joyful too, and wild like a song. And then she said, "Hawk told you to go home. Go HOME! Stop wandering. GO BACK TO YOUR PLACE! Hawk screamed to you. Claim your ground! Claim the Earth! GO HOME!"

It is easy to feel grounded and connected in the group after sharing and living together at such a deep level. But the group cannot stay together. Everyone must return to their lives. Everyone must take back to their home communities what they have learned. Angelo and Emerald cautioned us about telling the vision quest story too soon, or too often, or telling it to someone who isn't respectful or open, who may dismiss it.

They said that each of us should anticipate a loss of vision, a sadness that comes when we realize that most of the rest of the world does not know and does not care what triumph we experienced in the desert. We each may lose our own trust in our story.

Then Angelo told the story of a woman who came to fast. Like me (perhaps like you) she was a skeptic. She railed against the vision quest, against her decision to take part in it. In the circle she charged Angelo and Emerald with being charlatans. Her relationship with the group and the fast went on this way until after the mirroring process. At the closing council Angelo invited each person to say whatever they had left to say to the group. When this woman's turn came, it was obvious that something had shifted in her. She said simply, "This shit is real."

You want to know if the vision quest changed my life. You want to know if a vision quest will change yours. You will have to walk that road for yourself, of course. I can tell you that my story in the desert is now part of everything I do, everything I say, everything I see. I can't now imagine my life without it.

An Inside Passage

It is, however, fine indeed to know that if you've lost something
very good in your life it's still possible to go looking for it.
JIM HARRISON

"Keep moving unless you're not going anywhere!"
TSA OFFICIAL, Denver International Airport

In Fairbanks, that second night, a madness took me. I was restless.
Lonely. Angry at the sun that would not set. It was 2:00 a.m. and I
had pitched my tent next to the woodpile outside Billie's Backpackers
Hostel. I unzipped my down sleeping bag and lay sweating in the northern summer, my right leg kicked out, listening to the rain. I should
have fallen to sleep, I was so tired. But you know how rain can capture
you in a tent, how that loud popping sound against the taut fly plinks
at your brain, and wilts and loosens the fly as it rains, which bends in
on you, bends in on you until the fly and tent meet and rain begins to
drip through and down onto your precious down bag, onto your dry
clothes, onto your books and notebooks, which you hurry to return to
the waterproof bag you carry them in, and then runs in long lines, the
rain does, down the nylon seams to your feet and soaks your last good
pair of socks, even while you realize that the one thing you forgot to

do before leaving the dry country was seal the seams on your tent because ten years had somehow gone by since last you did it. Inside that damp envelope illuminated green by the northern night a rage grew up in me. I couldn't help myself. I cursed the sun, cursed that bright orb visible through the rain clouds and the thin veil of my shelter. I cursed Alaska and the stupid lost feeling I had, that little boy feeling that creeps in when you're sad and starts you wondering if you'll ever be strong enough, brave enough, happy enough to claim a home anywhere in the world. If you'll ever stop wandering. If you'll ever stop doubting and believe in yourself. If you'll ever say "I love you" to anyone except your dog, and mean it.

I pulled on my worn Arborwear pants—the only brand I wear these days—that and my GORE-TEX shell over a polypro T-shirt. Outside my tent now, I stood a moment in the rain. It wasn't raining hard, really, and I almost came to my senses. But no—that anger felt good, it felt powerful, reckless—and I removed all my worldlies from the tent and tore it down, wadding it into a weird, soggy baguette that I managed to fit inside the stuff sack. I tossed it all into the back seat of my rental car and sped off.

Where was I going? I didn't know. Out on College Road a few neighborhood children were riding their bikes. A couple walked the sidewalk, joined at their hands. I saw someone working over a flowerbed in the front yard of a house. Didn't people sleep in Alaska? A stray dog crossed in front of me and then looked back as if I had interrupted something. I was going nowhere, and my eyes hurt from needing to be shut. I drove aimlessly for awhile longer, maundering about until perhaps an hour had passed, and I parked the car, quite suddenly, in the empty lot at Pioneer Park. I was going to sleep in the car, but this was a trick because I knew I wasn't going to sleep in the car. I reclined the driver's seat and closed my eyes. Though I wasn't cold I pulled my sleeping bag out and tried to get into it, wrestling with the steering wheel in my way. I lay there, half in, half out, with my eyes open. An hour later I checked into a room at the Golden North Motel, pulled the draperies closed to make an artificial night, and fell asleep on the bed.

I was born in Fairbanks, Alaska, at the Fort Wainwright Army Hospital, on May 22, 1969. My father was a U.S. Army officer just out of the

ROTC program at Michigan State, and his deal with the devil was that in volunteering for Vietnam he would earn the right to choose his next station before getting shipped out. He chose Alaska. At that time Alaska had only been a state for ten years, and it was still considered a foreign post by the Army. So my father and mother were inoculated for bubonic plague, among other things, and traveled north with their first child, my sister, Rebecca.

When I was five months old and enjoying an Alaskan infancy, my father was called up for service in Vietnam. He packed up his young family and we started out on a journey that would keep us traveling for the next seven months. All told, we covered ninety-five hundred miles, mostly in a Dodge station wagon towing a tent trailer. We traveled from Fort Wainwright to central Michigan, where my parents had grown up and still call home; central Michigan to Fort Bragg, North Carolina (for military training); Fort Bragg to central Michigan (for Christmas); Michigan to Fort Bliss, Texas (for military training); and Fort Bliss back to Michigan, where during the month of my first birthday my father boarded a plane for the war.

Our way out of Alaska was in part a water journey, down the Inside Passage aboard the newly commissioned motor vessel the *Malaspina*. Newly commissioned because, like the state itself, the Alaska Marine Highway System had just appeared on the scene and the *Malaspina* was the first of three ferries to open service between the northern ports at Haines and Skagway and the southernmost port at Prince Rupert. Over the next fifty years the system would grow to nine motor vessels serving thirty-three ports over a route of thirty-five hundred miles, extending from Puget Sound to as far out the Aleutian chain as Dutch Harbor on Unalaska. The *Malaspina* would grow, too, taken into dry dock in 1972 to be renovated and lengthened—today the vessel is 408 feet long and spreads 74 feet at the beam, with a gross tonnage of 2,928. The *Malaspina* can board 700 passengers and up to eighty-eight vehicles. Its seventy-three staterooms sleep 238 passengers—the rest find seats or floor space in the various open lounges or on the back deck.

These tedious details are of interest to me because I have no memory of the journey or the *Malaspina*. I have no memory of Alaska. I realize now that I also have no memory of my father's departure. I wonder, though, how it may have determined my life, as any enterprise of pitch and moment will. I wonder now how every experience I had in that delicate stage—before the body has really decided it belongs in the physical plane—transformed me. I wonder, because so much of Alaska is in me.

For example, how is it that I am a morning person, rising instinctively at 4:00 a.m., usually without an alarm clock? Is it something that got into me in Alaska, something about the seasonal rhythm of light and dark that defines the far north, so that the rules of dusk and dawn at the temperate zone do not apply to me? And how is it that I'm a water person, when all of Alaska is braided in frozen and flowing water and the great coastline wanders through the Gulf, the Bering, the Chukchi, and the Beaufort seas? For all those hours shipboard as a baby, when I was surrounded by water, and water birds, and mammals of the sea, while the *Malaspina* swelled and sank with the tides marching over the border into Canada and on to the Lower 48. "My birthday began with the water—," announces Dylan Thomas in "Poem in October." How is it that I am a wanderer, when at five months old I embarked on a land journey crisscrossing North America for months? Did this early journey define my life? Did I spill over into a kind of addiction to the rhythms of passage, the way, say, a crying baby is soothed and softened by movement, by the cradled rhythm of the mother who lifts and dances it?

Which brings me to a bit of hack theory, or, at its best, poetic dispensation. British travel writer Bruce Chatwin spent his life interrogating "the nature of human restlessness." He came to believe, very deeply, as he writes in *The Songlines*, that "Natural Selection has designed us—from the structure of our brain-cells to the structure of our big toe—for a career of seasonal journeys *on foot* through a blistering land of thorn-scrub or desert." In this spirit, he discovered, "travel [is] not a curse, but a cure for melancholy: that is, for the depressions brought on by settlement." This is why, Chatwin believes, "greener pastures pall on us," and "possessions exhaust us," and Abel, the wandering herder, was favored by God. This is why babies stop crying when you pick them up and walk them about a room, because for the many thousands of years before agriculture, human beings lived on the move. We were no-mads: "What, then, are a nomad baby's first impressions of this world?" Chatwin writes. "A swaying nipple and a shower of gold." And so "the action or rhythm of walking was used as a technique for dissolving the attachments of the world and allowing men to lose themselves in God."

Walking is a holy act, he boasts, and, as Kierkegaard wrote, "if one just keeps on walking, everything will be all right."

Chatwin had a penchant for other modes of travel, too, though he saw going on foot as the purest form. While I am a walker of the most dedicated sort, I mean here to draw attention to travel in general. By travel I do not mean going on vacation, or even touring foreign cities and ruins. I mean consistent, ongoing movement, where the idea of home shifts from a fixed place (or was never present in this way to begin with) to a place the traveler carries inside. Time, too, is different for travelers than it is for settlers. For travelers, time is measured or mapped upon space. The past is the *place* you left behind (rather than a moment left behind), the present and future are *where* you are now and *where* you will be (rather than when). For travelers this difference gives rise to the illusion of exchanging time for space, of escaping time, even of the possibility of immortality. Travel can be a way to deny growing older, which is why there are so many stories of heroic travelers in search of immortality—the holy grail, the fountain of youth, or, in the case of Gilgamesh, how to overcome death. Einstein's Special Theory of Relativity corroborates this premise (and this is *not* hack theory). "Time was assumed to be absolute, regular and universal," writes Simon Singh in *Big Bang*. "No, said Einstein: time is flexible, stretchable and personal, so your time may be different from my time." Extraordinarily, but truly, if you were to travel close to the speed of light on a journey away from the Earth to the center of the galaxy, time would slow down immensely for you. It would take, by Carl Sagan's authority, about twenty-one years to reach your destination but about thirty thousand years would have passed on Earth. Theoretically, then, a kind of immortality is possible simply by going on a journey. Einstein went on to announce that space and time are inseparable, hence the term "spacetime."

But what does it mean? I think it means that because of this special quality of spacetime, whether you are aware of this quality or not, travel can be addictive. In such a condition, one *must* keep on walking for everything to be all right.

I'm not sure what I was looking for—perhaps I was in search of a story—but for years I have thought to make a journey to the place of my birth.

On June 27, 2006, I boarded the *Malaspina* in Bellingham, Washington, to retrace part of the route of my long-ago exodus. Most of all I wanted a water journey, and I thought just to enter Alaska would be enough. My plan was to live on the ship for four days, get off at its terminus at Skagway, stay for a few days, then take it back south. The *Malaspina* had been in service for longer than my lifetime, and my first sight of her was at dockside, the bold blue hull complemented by the white lettering announcing her name over the loading doors.

Her name, Malaspina, belongs to a glacier located in southeast Alaska between Mount St. Elias and the sea. Considered the largest glacier in North America, Malaspina Glacier measures some fifteen hundred square miles, larger than the state of Rhode Island—yes, still larger, despite these globally warmer times. The glacier, too, has a source for its name: a Spanish captain, later admiral, Don Alejandro Malaspina (1754–1810), who explored the coast of Alaska at the close of the eighteenth century in search of (among other things) a strait that would link the Pacific and the Atlantic, the fabled Northwest Passage. Upon seeing the mountain and its great glacier, Tomas de Suria, an artist traveling with Malaspina, wrote in his journal, "this was a piece of the coast which, except for the great mountain of St. Elias . . . is not known to have been seen by any traveler."

The *Malaspina* felt virginal to me, too, despite stepping aboard for the second time, for when the fellow at the ticket gate greeted me and asked if I'd ever sailed on the ship before, I had to say, "Yes." He looked over my boarding pass and my Texas driver's license (which is where I'd been living and teaching for the past year). "Texas, huh?" he queried. "So, then, welcome to the biggest state."

Shipboard, as we pulled away, the wind came up on the back deck, where like a few dozen other travelers, I had duct-taped my tent to the steel-sheeted floor. The tents fluttered violently in the cross-wind, yellows and reds, greens, pale opals and grays, so that the space held an air of festival and adventure, even some taste of sudden, though temporary, community, as travelers began to share their stories.

It was here I met Kay Kudo, who was securing her tent next to mine. Her truck was below on the car deck; she planned to drive from Haines to Fairbanks, where she had a new job fighting fire for the BLM. She would be stationed at Fort Wainwright. She had fought fire out of Tahoe for the Forest Service for more than a dozen years, but resigned after a dispute with her superior about the safety of her crew. Still claiming the Sierra as home, she expressed some reservation about living in faraway Alaska. And yet, living in faraway anywhere is part of the firefighter's life, as crews are called up and shuttled around the country where they are needed. As it turned out, Kay spent most of that summer fighting fire back in the Lower 48.

Fairbanks, I thought. Perhaps a water journey was not enough. Perhaps I should travel all the way to the source.

Later, satisfied that my tent was secure, I made my way forward to starboard to stand in the sun and wind. As we passed Point Roberts just south of Vancouver and pushed north up the Strait of Georgia, I met Simonette, a Filipino nurse from Los Angeles. She stood at the railing, as I did, watching the dark ocean that revealed none of its secrets. She wore a short skirt exposing her brown legs, and her bare arms were goosed by the sharpening wind. Her Asian hair was jagged at the ends, with bangs above her eyes and the remnant angle where once she had worn it short, like a boy. I suppose it was her delicate form that drew me, and then, as the journey grew into a day, and then two days, it was her wit and good company. At the railing, some small pleasantries went between us. I reported I had traveled in the Philippines, and we talked around that, before returning to watching the water and the bank-side verge for surfacing porpoises or whales before the cold pushed us indoors. By the time we reached Sitka, where Simonette was to work for the next three months, I came to know that, like me, something compelled her to travel.

Simonette was born in Dumaguete City in the Visayas, and spent most of her childhood in a village on Mindanao, the same big island that, these days finds its way into American newspapers. In 1995, after four years in nursing school in Manila, Simonette moved to Los Angeles to work in a nursing home. Her mother had already established herself in L.A., also taking advantage of the nursing shortage in American hospitals. But even before that caretaking was part of Simonette's everyday life. Her father is a doctor, and after practicing in Germany in the late 1970s he returned to the Philippines to establish a clinic with a few inpatient beds. Since he and his family lived in the same building that housed his clinic, Simonette's early memories are of the daily business of caring for the sick and injured. But she didn't feel called to the work out of a desire to do good, or even out of habit, she told me. Rather, nursing was a means to a steady, dependable income and the opportunity to move to the United States.

Sometime later she realized that financial stability was not enough. She tired of the routine of nursing and began to regard her work and daily life as generally miserable. "Then I saw traveling nurses who have all these stories about the places they've been and that was when the thought of traveling entered my mind," she told me. "I then had a goal. In April of 2002 I started my first travel assignment and have never stopped since." Her new life has taken her to a number of places in California and to Connecticut, Alaska, Washington DC, and the Virgin Islands.

What does it mean to be native to a place? To call a place home, to claim yourself of that place? Does birth give you the right? Does living your formative years in a place give it to you? Does working in a place? Does dying?

Kiowa writer and Pulitzer Prize winner N. Scott Momaday writes in "The American West and the Burden of Belief" that when Europeans arrived in North America five hundred years ago, "it was the home of peoples who had come upon the North American continent many thousands of years before, who had in the course of their habitation become the spirit and intelligence of the earth, who had died into the ground again and again and so made it sacred." If this is the definition of "native," I have no hope of being native to any place. My lineage is so scattered and disparate that such a place consecrated by the blood of my ancestors, even as it must exist, will never be found; I won't find it, anyway. Of my ancestry I know very little. On my mother's side I am Danish. On my father's side I am German and English. I'd rather like to claim my Danish heritage (to claim Hamlet as kin) but how can I when I've spent all of five days in Denmark during a youthful solo tour of Europe? Beyond that, my parents were raised in central Michigan and traveled west to Oregon in their early twenties. The greater Pacific Northwest is as close as I can get to defining a native ground, and I haven't lived there in twenty years. I *have* lived in twelve different states and one foreign country; in establishing myself in those places

I moved at least thirty-five times. (By "moved" I mean that I packed all of my worldly possessions in boxes, sealed them, put them on a truck or a plane or a ferry, and unloaded them into a different dwelling.) I've done a fair bit of wandering too—in addition to the twenty-eight U.S. states I have traveled or lived in, I claim Canada, Mexico, Japan, China, Korea, Philippines, India, Morocco, Spain, Italy, Greece, France, Austria, Switzerland, Germany, Czech Republic, Sweden, Denmark, and England, Scotland, Wales, and Ireland among the places I've traveled. Yes, there are people who have traveled or lived in more places than I, but this list is enough to back me up when I say that I'm not sure where home is.

My Cherokee friend Charlie Duncan, who leads sweat lodge ceremonies at his home in northern California, charges the people in his lodge to "become indigenous." Charlie was fond of saying, "This is an all-nations lodge. Everyone is indigenous to somewhere." To become indigenous, as Charlie puts it, does not mean to appropriate or idealize American Indian culture, and it does not mean that you should wear on your sleeve the rumor that someone in your family was an Indian (or so you think you recall hearing once over the holidays, but you can't remember who said it, that your great-grandmother might have told someone who then told your mother's mother that your great-great-uncle so-and-so might have been an Indian, or that he married an Indian, probably from a horse culture, which is why you loved horses as a child). No. What Charlie means is that everyone is human. Human beings evolved on Earth. And every human being is therefore entitled to a relationship with the Earth, with place and community. If you don't have such a relationship, it's time you re-imagined yourself, it's time you fell in love with a place and claimed a home there. It is Charlie's belief that "becoming indigenous" is an essential part of becoming a good steward of the land and of human communities. "Becoming indigenous" means becoming a human being. I trust this view, and I was greatly relieved the first time I heard Charlie speak about it. There was hope for me, I thought. By his reckoning I could discover or create a home for myself. I could claim a native ground.

Night came to day on the Inside Passage, and I woke to high peaks and snow, fishing boats and islands, and heavy wind troubling my tent. The resplendent sun pulsed on, then off the back deck, before retreating beyond the heavy gray clouds. I lay a moment inside the sound of the wind before determining that I felt no compulsion to battle it. I packed up my kit and moved in under the solarium near the bright yellow door that read "High Voltage."

It was still early, and only one other person stirred: Jim Porter, who had grown up working on his father's fishing boat out of Ketchikan. He had spent the winter and spring crabbing in Washington, and was on his way back home to fish the summer season with his father. He stood into the wind, his feet apart at shoulder width, a steady, boatman's stance. I came up beside him and stared out at the gray-black water. He pointed to one of several log barges. "You know how those work?" he said, befriending me. "They load 'em to the top, and then offset the ballast so they heel over. All the logs just pour into the water." He wore a hoodie over his head. Thick curly black hair stuck out around the edges, and he was missing a few front teeth. "Fishing season opens tomorrow, you know," he offered. "That's why all these seiners are jammin' up the Passage." The *Malaspina* was faster, however, cruising north at about 16 knots. "Hey! See those two boats over there?" Jim pointed out. "I know them. They're father and son. That old man is probably seventy-five, and he still outworks all the young guys. It's when they quit fishing that they get old real fast. 'Cause they have nothing to do. If they keep fishing, they stay young."

The *Malaspina* passed fishing boat after fishing boat, and the morning hours slipped by as the back deck woke up. Small groups of travelers, strangers really, formed and dissipated around conversations, card games, long bouts of shore-watching. People came and went from the shower facilities, the mess, the forward observation deck. The social dynamic shifted throughout the day depending on who was where, when. People fit into rough categories of purpose: Jim was local traffic, Kay and Simonette were job-bound and from somewhere else. There were two retired seamen: a Coast Guard officer who had lost his foot twenty years prior while stationed in Ketchikan (this was his first trip back); and a Naval careerman on vacation with his wife, who spent most of the voyage rail-side, hunting birds with a spotting scope. Then there was a young idealistic couple, Jared and Leonie, on their way to Haines to visit friends from a former Alaskan adventure, and an eighty-seven-year-old woman traveling with her son, seemingly at home everywhere, whose perspicacity impressed me immensely. Later, in the Recliner Lounge, I talked to a woman who had grown up in Anchorage. She was on her way back after several years in the lower 48. She wanted to test the idea that Anchorage could be her home again.

"Well, then," I told her, "you're a real native of Alaska, since you grew up there."

"No," she said. "You're the native, since you were born there."

Near the noon hour, Kay joined me at the railing. Her long wavy hair was wet from the shower and she dipped Skoal and spit into a plastic bottle. She was compact, road-toughened, and steady and honest-looking around the eyes. As we talked I noticed that she couldn't seem to stand still. She was here and then there, off greeting someone and then returning to the railing, leaning over to look into the sea, then back to catch me in the eyes, spitting expertly into the bottle. As she flittered about like a bird, we somehow kept a conversation that depended on two points: 1) Kay's father is Japanese (her mother, white American), and I had lived and taught for two and a half years in northern Japan; and 2) Kay had worked for some years for the U.S. Forest Service, and my father had put in thirty-four years with that same outfit. She asked me about what I knew of Japanese men. What kind of husbands are they, she wondered? How are ethnic differences overcome in a relationship? Are differences in ethnicity as challenging as differences in lifestyle— mobility vs. sessility, for example? Would she and her boyfriend last, as her father and mother had not? I had no answers, but returned her questions with questions of my own. Did she think a wandering life was prohibitive to a sustainable relationship? Did long-distance relationships result in weaker or stronger bonds between couples? Families? Friends? Would she ever give up her work to be with the man she loved? All of the scenarios, I told her, were part of my story, too, part of the struggles I'd had in my marriage, part of the impetus behind my divorce. The freshness and honesty of our conversation, as I took it, was not confessional or even evidence of two people who had "hit it off." Rather, it is a characteristic of traveling people: out here in motion on the road, the Self is no longer bound by the social conventions of home. Life is simplified, reduced, made pure, and honesty and vulnerability transform from weaknesses or weapons to commonplace characteristics of all human beings. On the back of the *Malaspina*, a neutral and temporal world, we could both recover our essential uniqueness and freedom and we could admit to each other that our fundamental natures were the same.

A woman whose name I never learned joined us. She was on her way home to Fairbanks, she said, after spending the past year caring for her ailing mother in faraway California. She looked hard-traveled. Her skin was ashen and folded more violently than her age demanded. Earlier that morning, as I sat up in my sleeping bag, I had observed her pouring herself a drink from a little bottle before tucking back in for a few more hours of sleep. She expressed relief in her mother's death. "Oh, I don't mean to be cruel, you know," she said. "I loved my mother to death. But I have a life, too, you know. And I'm real happy to be going back home."

I told her my story, why I was on the *Malaspina*.

"You're only going to Skagway?" she asked. "Oh, you must go to Fairbanks. The best little town in the world. You must. How can you get so close and not go all the way? Not travel to the place of your birth? Sometimes these opportunities are laid before us and we must take advantage of them," she said. "It might be risky, but you'll feel better about it if you do."

"Risky?" I asked.

"Shit, yes," she said. "It's always risky. You know how I got to Fairbanks?"

"How?" Kay asked.

"I followed my man up there. I was kinda down and out, you know. This guy asked me to come up and live with him, and I said yes. I sold everything down in California. Had just a few dollars to my name. I didn't intend to stay for more than a few months. You know, until I got back on my feet. But that was twenty years ago. That love didn't last. I moved out of his house pretty quick after. But I got me a better lover—Alaska." She became thoughtful then, self-absorbed, as if she were reliving the events of her life. And then she said, "And when you get to Fairbanks, you must go to the museum at the university. They got a polar bear there, right at the entrance there, that will knock your socks off."

The *Malaspina* started across Queen Charlotte Sound, the only real open water of the journey. Here the little ship began to rise and plunge in the higher seas, and I had to grip the railing to keep my feet. "Whoa!" someone shouted. The back deck sprang to attention as three humpback whales came into view to starboard. We watched them blow once, twice, three times, and then the glassy roll of their backs, and then the tails.

After the whales, my conversation with Kay shifted, became even more relaxed, as if somehow the whales had transformed us from fellow travelers to friends. Somewhere near Cape Caution, Kay agreed to give me a ride to Fairbanks.

On the menu in the mess my second night shipboard was chicken adobo, a Philippines standard, as most of the kitchen staff were Filipino. Like Simonette, they had capitalized on an opportunity and a number of them now lived in Juneau. "It's not the same," Simonette declared of the dish. "It's not the same adobo I know from Philippines. But I got it free anyway," she said, smiling.

The story was that the night before she woke to a knock at her cabin door. One of the crew had fallen ill, dehydration and vomiting. A passenger who had presented himself as a medical doctor wanted to administer an IV, but he could not get the needle in properly. From the ship's manifest they discovered a nurse onboard, and called on Simonette. She did what the doctor could not, and the captain rewarded her for her kindness with a meal ticket.

We took our time at the table, talking easily, deliberately, as the ship passed through the narrow Princess Royal Channel and on into Grenville Channel. The closeness of the banks encouraged silence on the ship, and the gangways filled with passengers eager to stand at the railings for a look. Eagles landed and rose from the tidal flats, and the sun came in low on the horizon. From the table in the mess I could see the trees, mostly western hemlock and Sitka spruce, running up the hard-rock mountains at such steepness as only sin could stick. We finished our adobo watching Canada pass by, and then we, too, went outside to enjoy the light, the birds, and the evening.

After saying good night to Simonette, I passed through the Recliner Lounge on my way to the solarium. Peter Jackson's *King Kong* was playing on a tiny little screen, but not a seat in the room was empty. *Isn't that odd*, I thought, climbing into my sleeping bag, *all these people here making a voyage on a ship while watching a movie about people making a voyage on a ship.*

In Ketchikan, passengers embarked and disembarked. And in that easy way that passage makes strangers into friends, destinations make friends into strangers. No one seemed to say good-bye. At ports at Wrangell, Petersburg, Sitka, Juneau, and finally Haines, new people appeared on the back deck and people I had become familiar with, disappeared. These new travelers, however, did not mix with those of us remaining who had boarded in Bellingham. They kept mostly to themselves. Or was it that we, the original group, did not allow them in? *Origin does bear weight,* I thought. Even in this fluid definition of place—the back deck of the *Malaspina*—relationships were determined by when and where.

A few hours before we arrived in Sitka, I sat with Simonette on the cabin deck, the lowest level of the ship accessible to passengers. We watched the land and sky as the engines carved a path in the sea under us. Idle talk was all we were up to. Just idle talk, when a young couple appeared with a baby. The mother held the baby in a cloth chest sling, and the father kept reaching out for it, placing his hand on its head, its back, over its tiny shoulders. It was asleep, that was clear, its eyes closed, its cheek pressed in against its mother's breast, the sling riding up around it to hold its head. The mother stood next to the railing, jogging a little up and down in a rhythm to keep the baby moving, to keep the baby happy. She had to turn sideways to lean out and over a little, to see into the great deep where life on Earth began. The baby, suspended like that, was in no real danger of falling, but beyond the railing there was no more ship if it did fall, only sea, the long blue passage of waters running the length of the continent.

And there I was, I thought. *I was that baby.*

I approached the couple and asked, How old?

"Five months," its mother said. "She's just five months old."

I told them my story, aware that the baby was "listening," that at five months old I, too, had traveled on this very ship. And now I had returned, I told them, on a journey back the way I had come. They roused to the idea of it, smiled and thanked me for telling them. Wouldn't it be wonderful, they said, if their tiny girl one day returned to the *Malaspina* in search of some original moment?

The encounter somehow completed me, as if I had journeyed back to know myself in transit from one self to another.

At Haines I jumped aboard Kay's Toyota pickup and off we flew north, up the Alcan and over the border into the Yukon. Somewhere south of Beaver Creek we pulled over to gawk at a black bear shambling off the road and into the bush. It was generally unconcerned about us, completely at home, making its way to wherever it was going. That was that, but when Kay pulled back onto the highway, it became clear that the rear driver's-side tire had gone flat. A nail or some sharp thing at the side of the road? It wasn't long before we had swapped it for the spare, and in Beaver Creek the tire man announced the flat was not reparable. The shop in Tok, he said, might be able to match a new tire.

We had a couple hours of road ahead of us with no spare for the spare, but the worst of it was that Kay would have to shuck out a hundred bucks or more for a tire.

"Just what I need right now," Kay said. "It's a disgusting habit, of course. And I hate it. I need to quit. But right now, I need a chew. And you're going to chew with me."

"No way," I said.

"Yeah," she said. "You gotta have a chew with me."

Kay bought a can of Skoal at the service station, forced a big dollop between her cheek and gum, and handed me the can. I suppose we had Skoal in common, too. Though I'd never chewed (except that one time when I was seven), my father had chewed Skoal for years before knocking the habit sometime in his late forties. In those days he ventured a single bumper sticker on his beloved Dodge truck that read: "Skoal Brother."

I took the can, aware that once again I was knocking about my origin. I pinched the slightest portion I could and slipped it into my bottom lip. Kay handed me a plastic soda bottle all my own, to spit in, and we were off again, traveling the good road and chewing together and laughing.

"We'll probably have to stop soon," Kay said plainly. "'Cause this stuff makes you gotta shit."

Only minutes had passed, a couple miles at the most, and I felt sick and drunk. The world was spinning around me and I thought I might not be able to hold on.

"How you feeling?" Kay asked.

"Man!" I said. "This stuff is brutal."

"I gotta pull over anyway," she said. "And maybe you need a break too."

A gas station rose out of nowhere and Kay pulled in behind an Alaska state trooper. I got out and stumbled a little, Skoal-drunk and woozy. The Trooper watched me all the way to the door. In the men's room I pulled the chew out and stood over the toilet to recover myself. I meant to put the chew back in, but I couldn't do it. I dropped it in and flushed it down.

A few miles down the road, Kay said, "Oh man, you took it out, didn't you?"

"Yeah," I said, feeling better. "That stuff is nasty."

"I thought we were havin' a moment here?" she said. "Christ, I'm gonna have to take away your man-card."

And so it came to pass that again I arrived in Fairbanks. I'd called ahead for a reservation at the Golden North Motel, and that's where Kay dropped me off. "Keep in touch," Kay said, the way you do to be polite. I agreed we should keep in touch, the way you do to be polite. Then I took up my gear and went inside.

That first day in Fairbanks was happy and full—a walking tour of downtown Fairbanks along the Chena River, a visit to the Golden Heart Plaza to see the bronze statue of "The Unknown First Family," lunch at the Second Story Café in Gulliver's Books, then on to the astonishing Museum of the North, and inside, "The Place Where You Go to Listen," an experiential "ecosystem of sound and light" installed by composer John Luther Adams. To finish it off I made an evening trip to the Malamute Saloon in Ester—a trip my parents had made before me—for a laughable musical review. At about 11:30 p.m. I turned in, anticipating a restful night in my tent aside Billie's Backpackers Hostel.

But no. Something, somehow, got into me. Something wild crawled in and drove me from the tent to the rental car to Pioneer Park and back to the Golden North, which is where I awoke, summer light pressing in against the window. Light, yes, but not sun. The sky was clouded over, threatening rain, and I felt an overwhelming desire to move on.

The urge was powerful, and it seemed to come from a deep place, a place I could not sound. "Could it be," Chatwin wrote, "that our need for distraction, our mania for the new, was, in essence, an instinctive migratory urge akin to that of birds in autumn?"

I returned the rental car and bought a ticket for Anchorage on the Alaskan Railroad. Within an hour I was seated in the dining car with a beautiful face bearing a faraway accent attending my full, hot cup of coffee—am I that shallow?—watching the Alaskan interior speed by the train windows. Somewhere along the Nenana the clouds finally broke and blue sky poured over the dark land. The interior of Alaska is dense, thick with an impenetrable ground cover of black spruce and standing water. How can even the great bear pass through it? Its skin and hair must be very hardy indeed to flourish in such a land as this. I loved it. I loved it. I loved it. Out here, in motion, passing through the land, I felt open and gregarious and free. All that manic energy drained away, and once again I felt settled and soft in my heart. Not meditative and sleepy, but awake, vital, alive. Shall I venture more Dylan Thomas?

> These were the woods the river and sea
> Where a boy
> In the listening
> Summertime of the dead whispered the truth of his joy
> To the trees and the stones and the fish in the tide.
> And the mystery
> Sang alive
> Still in the water and singingbirds.

Then I realized, speeding through the country that way, happier than I had been in days, that I had not even bothered to visit Fort Wainwright where my father was stationed and my mother birthed me. I had seen the space and fence around it from the highway but I had not bothered to approach the front gate, ask for a visitor's pass, something. Why not? It had hardly crossed my mind. Likely I would not have been permitted on base anyway, not with this new Army, this new military. The modern Fort Wainwright is probably forever entombed by America's hysterical fear of terrorism and the iron paranoia of the Department of Homeland Security. Was I born in a prison? Now that I was out, perhaps I had not the heart to go back in. Then I came to it, passing through the blithe country on the speeding train: It was not Fort Wainwright that I was after, nor Fairbanks itself, nor the Alaskan interior that completed me. It was the journey out of it. It was the passage to a new land. It was passage itself. The great gift my parents offered me was a baptism of movement, the bliss and rhythm of motion.

Winners of the River Teeth Literary Nonfiction Prize

Five Shades of Shadow
Tracy Daugherty

The Untouched Minutes
Donald Morrill

Where the Trail Grows Faint:
A Year in the Life of a Therapy
Dog Team
Lynne Hugo

The World Before Mirrors
Joan Connor

House of Good Hope: A Promise
for a Broken City
Michael Downs

The Enders Hotel: A Memoir
Brandon R. Schrand

An Inside Passage
Kurt Caswell

To order or obtain more information on these or other University
of Nebraska Press titles, visit www.nebraskapress.unl.edu.